CLASSIC
WILEY

BOOKS BY RALPH WILEY

Serenity: A Boxing Memoir

Why Black People Tend to Shout

What Black People Should Do Now

Dark Witness

BOOKS CO-WRITTEN BY RALPH WILEY

Best Seat in the House: A Basketball Memoir (with Spike Lee)

By Any Means Necessary: The Trials and Tribulations of the Making of Malcolm X (with Spike Lee)

Born to Play: The Eric Davis Story (with Eric Davis)

Growing Up King: An Intimate Memoir (with Dexter Scott King)

CLASSIC
WILEY

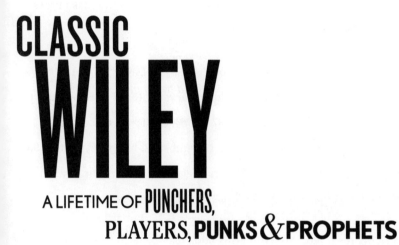

A LIFETIME OF PUNCHERS, PLAYERS, PUNKS & PROPHETS

RALPH WILEY

ESPN
BOOKS

ISBN 1-933060-01-8

Hyperion books are available for special promotions and premiums. For details contact Michael Rentas, Assistant Director, Inventory Operations, Hyperion, 77 West 66th Street, 11th floor, New York, New York 10023, or call 212-456-0133.

FIRST EDITION

10 9 8 7 6 5 4 3 2 1

CONTENTS

IMMORTAL YOUTH

GODS AND MONSTERS

BODY AND SOUL

THE MEASURE OF A MAN

FOREWORD BY
BOB COSTAS

Those of us who scribble a few lines on the pages preceding this collection of Ralph Wiley's finest work, remember him first as a colleague and a friend—vibrant, nimble-minded, and wryly humorous. He was also someone to be reckoned with. You knew he was in the room; not because he was loud, but because he was so damn interesting. If you were going to engage him in conversation, well then, you would have to keep up. And, once you gave it a try, you learned that while Ralph had strong points of view, he was also willing to honestly consider yours. He exuded self-assurance, but not the cheap posturing of someone who

IT WASN'T SO MUCH THAT RALPH REJECTED CONVENTIONAL WISDOM.

would rather lecture than learn. He was too intellectually honest to stoop to easy sentiment, but too decent to let easy cynicism trump compassion.

Ralph is rightly recalled as one of the first distinctly "black voices" in American sports media. As such, he provided perspective and shadings most others could not: giving voice to those who were historically un-represented or misrepresented. To acknowledge Ralph's role in America's evolving racial dialogue is fitting. But to let that alone define him is myopic. His race, his personal experiences, his natural affinity for the underclass and the underdog, *informed* just about everything he wrote, but they did not dictate what Ralph thought. His insight into the black condition was always part of a larger understanding of the human condition.

While it was clear which way Ralph leaned, you could never be sure exactly where he'd come down on any given issue. It wasn't so much that Ralph rejected conventional wisdom. He simply held it up to a different light. No matter how many others had addressed a particular topic, Ralph found a fresh way to look at it. With him, a sharp left turn off the path of orthodoxy was part of the ride. He was too independent to settle for the predictable narratives, or the standard poses of outrage that masquerade as edginess. If, in the course of speaking for himself, Ralph Wiley

HE SIMPLY HELD IT UP TO A DIFFERENT LIGHT.

spoke for you too—great. If not—well, let the debate begin.

In his newspaper columns, his magazine articles, his books, and his many television appearances, Ralph Wiley always had a message. His talent, his passion, and his presence made him a compelling messenger. In the pages that follow, you will find the best of what he delivered.

INTRODUCTION
MICHAEL WILBON

It was a boxing column I was particularly proud of writing. It was in the days before cell phones were ubiquitous, when voicemail had to do. I checked my messages back at home early on the Saturday morning of the big fight in Las Vegas and there was one from Ralph Wiley that was going to last four minutes. His voice was calm, as if he was starting the first day of a journalism class, which in fact he was.

He went through virtually each paragraph of my column, explaining why it was okay, why it was printable and fit for consumption, but why I hadn't written the best column I could write that day, why I'd left too much evidence on the table. He told me that day that good column writing was a calling, and each column was a sermon and it had to be carefully constructed to build to that point where even the doubters in the congregation were moved. I hadn't done my best from the pulpit that day, Ralph was saying. As the grandson of a southern Baptist preacher, I got that.

When the lesson by voicemail was over, I didn't know what to feel at first. I mean, I'd known Ralph since the very beginning of my career. I was 21 and he was 28, I think. But he seemed ten years older than that. In Vegas or Atlantic City, Ralph knew every lug in the gym who was taping fists or squirting water. He knew the ballplayers and the entertainers, every agent and every street runner for every agent. And he knew, even more importantly, how to manipulate the language, how to perfectly construct his argument and deconstruct yours. If he need-ed to be a southern Baptist preacher fine, and if he needed to deliver a little bit of Perry Mason, well that was okay, too.

Ralph didn't need me to solicit his opinion or his advice, and it did-n't matter if my tender feelings were hurt. When I first started writing a column for *The Washington Post*, on an occasional basis in the late 1980s, there were only two other black men writing general sports columns in the country. Ralph had left *The Oakland Tribune* and gone to *Sports Illustrated* by then, leaving Roy Johnson and Bryan Burwell holding the fort. The notion of racial inclusion hadn't yet reached the sports sections of daily newspapers.

The point is that Ralph didn't want any black columnists writing like chumps. Not even for one Saturday, not even for one early edition run if it could be avoided. Look, Ralph Wiley mentored a whole lot of people, black and white, men and women. But he was emotionally invested in what I wrote and how I executed it. And the same went for Burwell and Johnson, and a whole slew of others to follow, including William Rhoden of *The New York Times*, David Aldridge of *The Washington Post* and then ESPN, J.A. Adande, also of the *Post* and now *The Los Angeles Times*. I wasn't the only one get-ting calls, and this was before the internet, when the touch of one key enabled you to see what was being written from coast to coast.

But Ralph always had his own buttons to push. Sometimes, the voicemail message wasn't so warm and fuzzy. But there were some calls that were standing ovations, or so they felt like. And I can't think of too many people whose opinion mattered so much over time. If Ralph Wiley thought I had written a good column, then it was a good column, good enough for any pair of eyes. I know I construct a better column today because of him. I also know I write a big fight story better today because of Ralph, because the fight game always brought out the best in him. The Storyteller, whether we were in Las Vegas covering the trials for the U.S. Olympic team or Memphis covering Mike Tyson vs. Lennox Lewis. Ralph could give you 1,000 words you would never read anywhere else on the precision of Jerry Rice's pass routes as easily as a marine could drop to the floor and give you fifty. But he felt the fights in a way all the great sportswriters of the 20th century felt the fights.

He also felt the need to work—virtually all the time. Ralph was never "off." He didn't see the need for any real vacation time. On any given day he was filing a column, working on a chapter in a book that had a deadline next week, starting a script treatment, and talking to the publisher about another book.

Selfishly, I never minded that a knee injury prevented what might have been a promising football career for him because the world was much better off having Ralph to challenge widely held notions and what was thought to be prevailing wisdom. The business of journalism was much better off for having Ralph prove and provoke, agitate and annoy. There was nothing quite as enjoyable as Ralph making certain folks who thought they knew everything totally uncomfortable by turning polite conversation political.

He accepted nothing at face value and told those of us coming up behind him that if we did, we were fools and not worth the desk space our newspapers and magazines set aside for us. As the conversation raged in the late 1980s and early 1990s about the notion of black athletic superiority, Ralph wrote this passage in *Why Black People Tend To Shout:* "Are black people, all people of African descent but especially African-American men, naturally superior athletes? If you are asking me, I'd have to say not that I've noticed. But why ask in the first place? I want to know why black men have to be naturally superior athletes. If we are, it would inevitably follow that black men are naturally inferior at something else."

There are a whole lot of unqualified discussion leaders in the sports world, particularly now that there is twenty-four-hour coverage of it, nationally and locally. And I don't know that Ralph wasted his time with them, either listening or sparring verbally. But I do know I miss the nights talking with him before a big fight. I miss the voicemails especially, the ones that said, "Good job" and the ones that said, "Wilbon, that was a B-minus. You let this guy off the hook for ..." All of us should miss being challenged and pushed to be smarter and more discerning. It's a lot quieter out there without Ralph Wiley, and the silence is deafening.

IMMORTAL
YOUTH

GAINING ON A LEGACY

For a February 2004 column on minority ownership in sports, Wiley looked back on his career—from his early days at The Oakland Tribune *to his many years as a writer and editor at* Sports Illustrated—*to reflect on his journey, professionally and personally. And on how much work was still left to be done.*

I look forward. Occasionally, I look back to see how far we've all come, although looking back flies in the face of Satchel Paige's axiom: "Don't look back, something might be gaining on you."

Cute saying or ominous warning?

Both, probably. Depends on *how* you look back at it. Satch was a big-league pitcher all his life, but in a segregated league for most of it. He didn't pitch in a *completely* big league until he was well over 40 years old, back in 1948, when he went 6-1 for the World Champion Cleveland Indians.

Now, did Satchel gain on big league baseball? Or did it gain from him?

Over fifty years later, I've come to think, and believe, that the final frontier in the American sporting republic is Total Ownership. I don't mean to say "minority" ownership. I look forward to the day when "minority" ownership returns to its pure, Econ 101 meaning—when it refers only to someone who owns a portion of any given team that is less than a fifty-percent stake.

As human beings, *homo sapiens*, people, we all are individual, discrete. We all have our own talents, hopes, dreams, rights, and responsibilities under law and the U.S. Constitution, none of which should be rescinded or restrained except by our own individual talents, our conduct, and work ethic.

Total Ownership means everyone who participates in a meaningful percentage in a labor force is involved at all other levels, including majority individual team ownership, under the industry umbrella of Sports In America. Why is this important? That's our destination.

First, the journey.

When I began in sports journalism back in the late '70s as an off-shoot of the greater, growing industry of Sports In America, the landscape was different than it is today. I was considered by some to be a second-wave pioneer, to others, a nuisance. Luckily, I was oblivious to this history and currency, and it did not hinder me en route to later understanding. This was due to the good graces of the caretakers of *The Oakland Tribune*.

This might seem ironic, since I was a child of the Southern style of racial segregation and no doubt was naïve on certain levels because of it; and *The Oakland Tribune* had been historically a conservative, if not stiffly arch-conservative, newspaper. But such is the stuff, value, and utter nonsense of most political affiliations. They really mean nothing—not to an individual life, unless they happen to stunt it. They help people get elected, or become rich, by espousing certain popular views. They move units. But they don't stop life.

And life is progress. People who stand still are lost. Being blissfully ignorant of these and most other facts did not hinder me at all from applying for work as a copyboy. Neither, in the end, did it keep me from getting hired, nor did it taint the tuna fish sandwiches I brought from the small cantina across 13th Street for the lunch of Joe Knowland, heir to *The Oakland Tribune.*

Mostly, I showed up, and kept showing up. The caretaker editors of *The Tribune*, though they may have argued the wisdom of their decision, decided my good outweighed my bad. *The Tribune* was a small metropolitan daily that happened to cover five pro teams, three of which were stationed within a five-mile drive of the newspaper offices— the Oakland A's and San Francisco Giants; the Oakland Raiders and San Francisco 49ers; and the Golden State Warriors—as well as Stanford, Cal, St. Mary's, Santa Clara, San Jose State, and USF college sports teams.

There were a number of editors who helped me go from fetching tuna sandwiches to eating them. I recall the names even today: Roy Grimm and Fred Dickey; and the sports editors George Ross and then Bob Valli. They were all white—and all men, actually—and, to a man, they were all encouraging. Mr. Ross pointed out articles in *The Atlantic Monthly* or *Sports Illustrated*, saying, "This is *you*," and telling me about James Beckwourth, a 19th-century frontiersman of African, European, and indigenous blood who found the pass through the Sierras. George said Beckwourth might make a good story for me one day.

Or he'd just tell me of his fondness for the amazing abilities of Willie Mays, and also of his understanding of Mays, though many of Ross's contemporaries had a lesser opinion of Mays's persona. He was a noted sourpuss (see Bonds, Barry, and Williams, Ted, etc.). These editors helped give me what one needs to progress. Often, that is perspective.

All this because I had been allowed to write a story about Julius Erving joining the 76ers for the merger of the ABA and the NBA. This was for the *Trib*'s season-opening NBA package, the season after the Warriors won their first and only NBA title, in 1975.

Bob Valli would today be seen by anti-affirmative types, black and white, as controversial, if not notorious. He liked me. Or, rather, he liked what I wrote. Simple as that. So he took me—a tyro, this naïf, with my small helmet of an afro and my sporadic facial hair and a wardrobe out of Levi-Strauss and some T-shirt factory—and set me forth upon the sports world as a member of the Fourth Estate. After a suitable period cityside, covering the courthouse, night cophouse, city council meetings, retirement dinners, and bureaus, he brought me into Sports and sent me first to the New Oakland Boxing Club and eventually to all the big-money fights in Vegas.

He sent me to cover the Raiders, at first caddying for Tommy LaMarre, and then the 49ers. He sent me to cover USF basketball, Cal football, and Stanford, after John Elway arrived. He gave me the Giants' beat, where I became a card-carrying member of the BBWAA (Baseball Writers' Association of America) and learned the peculiar rhythms of 162 big-league games. He sent me on the road with the Oakland A's when Ron Bergman or Tom Weir needed a break. "Perilous Travels With Charlie" read the first headline after I wrote about a charter bus ride between Chicago and Milwaukee that occurred after the A's lost both ends of a double-dip on my first roadie. Jack McKeon was the manager, chief cook, and bottle washer for that team. He said, "You can't write about that!" but Valli seemed happy that I had. Let it be said that Trader Jack didn't say, "You can't write!" He said, "You can't write about *that!*"

Big difference.

The game was changing. I was already part of it. And Charlie Finley, sitting with his arms imperiously crossed across his chest behind home plate at Comiskey Park and whistling "Camptown Races" past the graveyard as I interviewed him, could not stop the brave new world from progressing on.

7

Behind two other editors named Henry Freeman and Bob Maynard, I ended up writing a column, as a columnist, about Finley's departure from baseball some three years later.

Finley sold out to the Haas family, of Levi-Strauss ownership fame. They were a pleasant—I almost want to say normal—family: the father Walter, the son Wally, geeked as all get-out about this turn of events (the chance to own a team!) and the son-in-law Ron Eisenhardt, who I termed then and still think of now as "Iron Man." The Levi-Strauss company itself was no longer the singular beneficiary of my new wardrobe budget.

At this stage, in my memory, not only were black and brown and female and Latino and Asian sports journalists rare, there simply were no black general managers or player personnel directors in football or baseball or basketball; and damned few head coaches.

It wasn't a question of having representative numbers. It was a question of having one number—one who'd show how smart it was in the long run.

I "covered" Al Attles of the Golden State Warriors, one of the first black head coaches. Actually, Al "covered" me, blessed me with decades of wisdom and knowledge. Al Attles was a gentleman of boundless good will and enthusiasm; he was glad to see me, happy to help me along my way in the craft. The Warriors won the NBA title in 1975 with Al as head coach. Following Bill Russell's title in 1969 as player-coach,

Al was the second black man to coach a world title.

Three years after that, Lenny Wilkens won one with the Sonics. Soft-spoken Bill Lucas briefly held a position of authority with the Atlanta Braves, a nebulous combination of personnel guru and GM without contract green-lighting powers. He died too young.

NFL head coach or coordinator wasn't even a consideration. Frank Robinson became the Cleveland Indians bench manager during the mid-'70s. On June 30, 1978, Larry Doby became the second black baseball manager, taking over the White Sox at the behest of a progressive owner named Bill Veeck—the same progressive owner who'd also hired both Doby and Paige in the first place back in 1948, once the reasonableness and profitability of that process had been initiated by Jackie Robinson and Branch Rickey under the aegis of Happy Chandler, commissioner of baseball.

I recently had dinner in the company of Bud Selig, who has continued a progressive tradition in his term as commissioner. History will remember him better than his current notices, moreso if the team his family owns, the Milwaukee Brewers, sells to an African-American majority ownership interest.

That is not necessarily up to him, but to the marketplace. Still, that transaction would join the Hispanic/Latino majority ownership of the Anaheim Angels as occurring on his watch and would make baseball the organizational model of full participation at all levels within the industry—except player agents.

Throughout the early days of my own career, I got some interesting reactions to my own modest yet undeniable place in the Sports in America spectrum. By the time I got to *Sports Illustrated* in 1982, reactions were sometimes tempered by the clout of the organization I represented. I was Ralph Wiley of *Sports Illustrated*. Big difference. Whatever negative reaction might have been, whatever joke might have been told, was held in abeyance, caught in the throat of the person being dragged into the future. Didn't make much sense to joke about someone who could then cut you a new one in print. In fact, I might not have been able to do that, or have even been inclined to do that; but that didn't stop the possibility.

Possibility is what's important, not the day-to-day fact of life at a magazine or a network or a pro team or a league. Day-to-day sausage-making is not always a pretty sight. Progress is not a pretty sight at first, although some of the vistas are breathtaking. I know I've often thought of James Beckwourth during these years.

In time, people in and out of the industry got used to me being here, part of the growth of my part of the industry and of the industry itself. I did several things within it, things you might say hadn't been done before. Some might not have liked it. Some of them do not like it still—maybe even you; or, if not you, then someone you know. But all these people within the range of even my limited influence know that their scope has been broadened. If they don't know this, at least they're easy to spot.

All this has been my long-winded way of making the point that Dr. Martin Luther King Jr. made long ago: If you integrate education, and media, everything else will follow. People doing the things they have the passion and capacity to do will no longer be seen as strange, or deviant, or somehow lessening the quality of production or society. In fact, production increases due to increased competition and ingenuity—unless you think it was an accident that *SI* won four or five Magazine of the Year awards during my time there, or that Raghib Ismail made out like a bandit and ushered in the era of NFL-style free agency, limited though it be.

Not that I was responsible for all of this. But I was part of the process. So new things were invented. New processes and ideas and access points were unveiled. This is the essence of progress.

The delivery of information has gotten better, and data itself is more in-depth, complete, intuitive, entertaining. The games have gotten faster; the athletes bigger, stronger, and faster; the industry itself has become a giant, and not simply "the toy factory." FAO Schwarz might be going out of business, but the NFL is in no danger of that. And despite their problems, neither is the NBA, NHL, or MLB. And I happen to believe this is no accident. The trick is not to stagnate.

Sports has become America's next great pseudo-manufacturing base. What is it that we make better than everybody? Spectacle.

Everything has gotten better in my twenty-five years in sports, at least along these social and production lines. Except this: total ownership. That filters down to everything—to the attitudes of the labor force itself, which can see who has been shut out of the owners' suites, and which may somehow take that to mean a black coach is not to be respected as much as a white coach. There are 100 similar dilemmas that hide under the umbrella What's Wrong With the Lack of Ownership Picture? That's the part of the picture that the Sports World can, and must, address.

To not progress in the area of individual team ownership, within the umbrella of all the leagues, would be hypocrisy. There have been fits and starts. In the NFL, Fritzie Pollard had a sort of deal with the Ohio team where he coached. That didn't last long; it was a simple aberration. Nothing since, not so much as a head coach until maverick owner Al Davis (who leveraged his way into an NFL ownership position not through acquired wealth, but with acumen and the ability to make himself essential to a team and half the league) hired the first "black" head coach, modern era. This was Art Shell, and as recent as 1989.

Ten years before that, Davis, for all his faults and litigious nature, had hired the first Hispanic-American NFL head coach, Tom Flores. Perhaps Davis understood, and was not bound by any unseemly—indeed, ungodly and pernicious— tenets of any exclusive Masters-like social club.

There is a long history of pro baseball ownership, notably in the Negro National League (founded 1920) of Rube Foster, but that history deserves its own telling. It petered out in the late '50s, with the final and complete integration of the big leagues.

In hindsight, merging the Kansas City Monarchs and Homestead Grays into the league along with select players might have been a good idea. But I suppose you have to crawl before you walk and sit, and I suppose you have to be noticed and appreciated before you are asked to dance.

There was a brief ownership position by African-Americans of the Denver Nuggets in the '80s; didn't last long because the GM of said team, who happened not to be African-American, signed a player on his way out to a massive contract. Peter Bynoe, the minority owner, then tried to talk to this player and his reps about re-doing the contract. They nearly fell down laughing. Nothing bad ever happened to the general manager in question, at least not relative to that ill-advised contract. At any rate, the minority owner decided this was a good time to get out. Nothing wrong with that. None of this has any real permanence, in terms of individuals. Owners, like coaches and players, will come and go in the end; things progress.

Once everybody is in the tent, at all levels of competition, the reality changes. It can be as simple as a joke that goes from being laughed at because it's so "true" to being unacceptable because it's so stupid. Not only do certain jokes become unacceptable, but also certain automatic whining about a perceived lack of opportunity or racism become unacceptable, too. The industry becomes what the on-field reality of sports always claimed to be: a true meritocracy.

That's a fitting legacy for Branch Rickey and Jackie Robinson, for Bill Veeck and Larry Doby. Hell, for that matter, for Bob Valli and Ralph Wiley. And more, too many to list— you and somebody you know, maybe, someone who helped you realize your legacy, a legacy that all of us, man, woman, black, white, brown, share in the panorama of American sports. Not in some distant future, but here, and now.

—*ESPN.com, February 12, 2004*

DOC &
DARRYL

Dwight Gooden and Darryl Strawberry were several years into their careers when Wiley profiled them for Sports Illustrated *in 1988, but they had already lived such full lives—on and off the field—that it was sometimes hard to remember just how young they still were. And while both men would face personal adversity in the years that would follow, there was still enough good baseball ahead of them—Mets catcher Gary Carter predicts Gooden will pitch a no-hitter one day— that Wiley was hopeful they would fulfill their great promise.*

The New York Mets came into muggy St. Louis last month in all their glory, leading everybody else in the National League East. The Mets are known as Kid and Mex, HoJo and Mookie, Nails, Mac, El Sid, and by some names that aren't so innocent. They're also known as a brash and arrogant collection of accused bat corkers, camera hogs, and huge egos. The Mets inspire such name-calling largely because they can lay claim to being the best baseball club on the planet, and there are at least two reasons that they probably will be able to make that claim well into the 1990s. They are Darryl Strawberry and Dwight Gooden, who are known as Straw and Doc, among other things.

Here are four ways to look at Straw and Doc:

The first is through the eyes of a former player. "Most guys have talent, but not that extraordinary talent, so people can't understand what those two have had to go through," says Tim McCarver, a Mets TV announcer and a major league catcher for 21 years. "Darryl and Dwight have had to mature under so many eyes. Yet they seem to have done it. Without them, the Mets are a good team. With them, it's not stretching it to say that the Mets are a great team."

The second way to look at Straw and Doc is through the eyes of an artist. "The similarities between them are amazing, aren't they?" says LeRoy Neiman, the popular painter and an unregenerate Mets fan. "They are the two I've drawn the most of all the Mets. The first time I saw Gooden, I didn't know who he was, but I knew he was somebody. Darryl has that, too. They both have a grace you can't express in words. I think they're the most extraordinary pair in baseball, in sports . . . ."

The third view is through the eyes of baseball's best handler of pitchers. "If I could have one player off the Mets' roster, it would have to be Gooden," says San Francisco Giants manager Roger Craig. "A guy who will go get you twenty wins [a year] for twelve years. He's got the perfect delivery for the split-finger. I'd talk to him about throwing it, but, believe me, I wouldn't insist."

The fourth is through the eyes of the best manager in baseball. "If I could pick one guy in all of baseball to start an expansion team with, it'd have to be Strawberry," says Whitey Herzog of the St. Louis Cardinals. "I'd put him at cleanup, get me six jackrabbits and a plumber to hit behind him, and I'd have myself a f_____ team. Strawberry's the guy."

Straw and Doc dress side by side in the visitors' clubhouse at Busch Stadium and then walk out into the sun and the gaze of curious fans. The previous evening, the lefthanded-hitting Strawberry, even though he was playing with a sore thumb, a strained groin muscle, and a tender hamstring, had driven in four runs, two on a monstrous home run off Cardinals left-hander Larry McWilliams, to lead the Mets to a 6-2 victory. The day before that, Gooden had won the game against the Chicago Cubs. In the bottom of the seventh, after having thrown a no-hitter to that point, he blasted a two-run homer to the back row of the bleachers at Shea Stadium and then ducked his head and sped around the bases, unable to suppress a childlike smile. In the next inning, Gooden lost his no-hitter and his shutout, but not the game, as the Mets won 11-3.

Who could have guessed a year ago that this is how things would be going at midseason of 1988? Back then, Gooden had recently been activated following a four-week stay at the Smithers Alcoholism and Drug Treatment Center in Manhattan, for rehabilitation from cocaine abuse, and a month in the minors. Strawberry was in the throes of a sepa-ration from his wife, Lisa, who had charged that he had beat-en her. He was also at odds with his teammates, some of whom had lambasted him publicly for missing two games in a key series with the Cards because, he said, he was ill. However, on one of those days he spent several hours publi-cizing a rap number he had recorded the day before. Both

Doc and Straw were victims of their own bad decisions.

In 1988, with the aid of each other and the passing of time, they have reassumed their star status as if they had simply taken a long coffee break. Each has changed—for the better. Gooden is now a precision pitcher in a power pitcher's body, while Strawberry, thanks to having developed more discipline at the plate, has finally begun to come fully into his own.

In his seven no-hit innings against the Cubs, Gooden threw only 74 pitches. "Better that way," he says. "I had good velocity. I was 96 to 97 [mph] on most of my fastballs, even though I didn't have my good stuff. Only threw one fastball that wasn't in the 90s, but the curve wasn't as hard as I'd like."

Doc then turns to Straw and asks, "Did it look like I had my good stuff?"

Strawberry teases him, tilting his right hand back and forth, as if to say, "Just so-so."

Straw gets on well with the Mets pitchers. In the Shea Stadium clubhouse, his cubicle is flanked by those of six pitchers, three on each side, and his best friend on the team, besides Gooden, is David Cone, the young righthander. Straw amused the entire staff early in the season by taking the mound during a workout in Montreal. How did he do?

"Well, Straw had good velocity. He was bringing it," says Gooden.

What about his control? Doc chuckles and says, "Bad."

Now, in St. Louis, the Cardinals are finishing batting practice.

Straw and Doc walk onto the field together and chat with Cardinals shortstop Ozzie Smith at the batting cage.

Ozzie: Say, Straw, what was that you did to us last night?

Straw: Aw, I just got a hanger, Oz. I just got a piece of it.

Ozzie: Pretty big piece. And what was that stance, that corkscrew?

Smith mimics the new stance Strawberry has been using this year, in which he lifts his right foot just before he swings, as Japanese slugger Sadaharu Oh did.

Straw: It helps the balance.

Ozzie: You don't need help. That home run only went about 10 rows back. And you, Doc, who was that you took deep the other day?

Doc: [Bill] Landrum.

Ozzie: So how's the curve doing?

Doc: Good. Real good.

Ozzie: Thanks, Doc. Thanks a lot.

Doc: Aw, Oz, you know I can't get you, anyway.

Strawberry and Gooden get down to business. Straw enters the cage and with an easy golflike swing hits one long drive after another down the power alleys. Doc lopes along in the outfield, casually shagging flies.

"In New York, if you move your fork on the dinner table, people read about it," says Smith. "So for them to excel is extraordinary, yet so natural. Right now, they're feeding off each other, not worrying about what other people think. It's a gift, being able to play like they can play. And now they're realizing that it's a gift. A Strawberry, a Gooden? Talentwise, they don't come along every day. It'll be my pleasure to say I played against them and beat them sometimes."

Straw and Doc wear the same size shoes, and each has a young son who carries his father's name. They also live within walking distance of each other in town houses on Long Island. However, despite their many similarities, Strawberry and Gooden are very different men.

Strawberry is outspoken. If he is hit, his first reaction is to hit back. He seems younger than twenty-six. The key to his success is the power in his arms, hands, and wrists. After five years in the major leagues, he's just beginning to realize his potential.

In late May, Straw is sitting in front of his locker at Shea as a driving rainstorm delays the start of a game against the Los Angeles Dodgers. Like lightning to a rod, ten or fifteen reporters converge on him, and he starts talking: "Really, I'm not to the point where I'm hot yet, and that's kind of scary . . . . I'm just starting to get it in my mind what I can do, not what anybody thinks I can do . . . . We're healthy, we're playing well, we're happy, and everybody hates us again."

Across the room is Lee Mazzilli, New York's thirty-three-year-old pinch hitter, known as Maz. Once he, too, was a young Mets star, but he didn't have as many good players around him. Nor did he have Strawberry's gifts. Mazzilli was one of the Mets who criticized Strawberry for sitting out those two games last year.

But seasons change. On June 13, Straw and Maz combined to end a Mets five-game losing streak, with a 2-1 win over the Cardinals at Shea. Strawberry touched McWilliams in the fourth inning, hitting a ball off the bullpen wall beyond right-field for his thirteenth homer of the season. Then Maz got the game-winner, a chop single over a drawn-in infield, in the twelfth inning. Strawberry was the first out of the dugout to high-five Maz as he crossed the plate.

"One thing that can never be rushed is experience," says Mazzilli. "Darryl has the most talent in baseball. But he was a kid. Now he can use that talent. To a certain degree, I went through that. I know the demands on him. I know there's no question that he has more talent than anyone I've ever seen. There's nobody even close. I'd like to have Darryl's talent just for one year, to see what I could do with it."

Another Met who has been outspoken about Straw is Keith (Mex) Hernandez, the thirty-four-year-old lefthanded-hitting first baseman and No. 3 hitter. In the April issue of *Esquire* magazine, in which Strawberry ripped several of his team-mates, he said of Hernandez, "Who the hell knows where his head was half the time last season." Mex is sitting on the bench in the dugout and makes a face when the *Esquire* story is mentioned. But Hernandez has respect for Straw. "For some reason, Darryl listens to me," he says. "I think it was the second half of '86 when he finally moved closer to the plate against lefties. Hey, everybody has to be shown. Ken Boyer showed me. Anyway, since then, Darryl's been a terror. An enforcer. Since [Jack] Clark left, he's the dominant hitter in the league."

"Darryl's comfortable up there," says McCarver. "He's hitting his pitch, going to left-center. He's showing he learned something from Keith. And one day, Darryl will hit a baseball farther than anyone has ever hit a baseball before."

Strawberry doesn't have far to go. Early this season he blasted a homer in Montreal's Olympic Stadium that, had it not hit a bank of lights near the roof, would have traveled an estimated 525 feet, just forty feet shy of Mickey Mantle's famous blow out of Washington's Griffith Stadium in 1953. And Straw has continued to hit the long ball. On Saturday, he hit his twentieth home run, his 11th against a lefty, to move ahead of the San Francisco Giants' Will Clark for the league lead. Through Sunday, he was hitting .301 with 53 RBIs.

"I've always been outspoken," says Straw. "I've said things, and I've meant what I've said. If you criticize me, I can criticize you. I had a real tough time in New York. I had to sit down and take a look at what life was all about. I feel proud of myself now, that I didn't let anyone run me out of town. But I had to go through experiences. I had to learn if I was strong. I am. I know it now."

Strawberry was already Gooden's model when they attended instructional league together in the winter of 1982, back when Straw was 20 and Doc was 17. "Doc was groomed like I was," says Straw, "to come up and dominate on the major league level." The next season, during spring training, Gooden, who would go 19-4 with 300 strikeouts in 191 innings in the minors that year, asked Strawberry, who would join the Mets in early May, if he could borrow his spikes for good luck. "I was so nervous," says Gooden. "He asked me, 'What size do you wear?' I said, 'Same as you.' I didn't really know. But turned out we both wore 11's. It was just fate."

"I had to throw Darryl before the public at an early age," says Mets media director Jay Horwitz. "From him I learned what not to do with Dwight. We had lost 97 games the year before Darryl came up. So he had to be the story."

After the 1986 season, the story turned grim. Strawberry now has 167 home runs, lifetime, the most in Mets history. But with that swing of his, says former teammate Kevin Mitchell of the Giants, "you kind of expect him to hit 20 home runs every game." In '86, Straw had 27 homers, but because of his talent, the press kept referring to his total as "only 27." That winter he became estranged from his wife and son. The separation was a failure of a most cutting nature for Strawberry, who had been raised in inner-city Los Angeles by his mother, Ruby, a single parent after his father, Henry, moved out when Darryl was thirteen. By the spring of 1987, he felt adrift. "I had to see if I wanted to lead a different kind of lifestyle," he says. "I found out that I didn't want that at all."

One evening during last year's All-Star break, as Strawberry stood outside the Hyatt Regency in Oakland, he was urged to enter a car by two beautiful women and their driver. It was a tempting offer, but Straw thought about what had happened to Doc and declined. Later, he stood by the hotel bar with a boyhood friend, Eric Davis of the Cincinnati Reds. They looked at each other and laughed the way two old friends who have made something of themselves can laugh without having to say anything specific.

Recently, quoting one unnamed source relying on information from a second unnamed source, The Cincinnati Enquirer linked Davis with possible drug use, a charge Davis vehemently denied. "If we weren't black, we wouldn't have to go through some of the things we go through," Strawberry says. "So what else is new? When you're younger, you think it's unfair, wrong. You get mad. You want to hit back. But how do you hit back against a label? Then, if you realize what's important in life, you accept that this is the way it is and go on about your business. How long does it take anybody to grow up, especially when we had to come up, with that talent, so quickly?"

Despite all the distractions, including harsh exchanges with teammates and manager Davey Johnson, Strawberry performed well in 1987. He hit 39 homers and drove in 104 runs, while batting .284. He also set club records for total bases (310), runs scored (108), and extra-base hits (76). On July 20, Johnson made Strawberry the Mets' clean-up hitter, and he played a major role in keeping New York in the division race until the last week of the season. He had come of age as a player.

By early fall, Straw and Lisa had reconciled. Lisa became pregnant, and on June 28, a daughter, Diamond Nicole, was born to the Strawberrys. Now most is right with Straw's world. Yet no one noticed that his resurgence began when Doc came back to the Mets. During his absence, Strawberry had worn the Doc's game pants. "No one knows how that touched me," says Gooden.

"I'm relaxed, not trying so hard," says Strawberry. "I know I'm going to hit. I don't know if Doc's coming back turned me around or not. Maybe it turned the whole team around. I've always thought that we're better than we think we are. And we think we're pretty good."

Gooden is quiet and sensitive. If hit, his first reaction is to avoid being hit again. He seems older than twenty-three. The key to his success is the power in his legs. After four years in the major leagues, it seems as if he has already done just about everything a pitcher can do, except throw a no-hitter.

"The no-hitter is just a matter of time," says catcher Gary Carter, a.k.a. Kid. "When Doc's got his breaking ball, I haven't seen too many people do much with him. The thing about Dwight is he's blessed with a strong body, strong legs. He could be great for a long time."

When Gooden speaks of pitching, there is a softness in his voice. "I always remember seeing things as a pitcher," he says.

"I went to watch the Reds in spring training when I was a boy growing up in Tampa. My father took me. He was always saying, 'Don't be afraid to throw the breaking ball when behind.' So in a way I've been pitching my whole life. Every time out, I learn more and more about myself. People can give you advice, but when you go out there on that mound, you're all alone."

To suggest that there is a softness about Gooden might seem ridiculous, yet there it is. The soft voice, the lack of pretension. "Straw's in a world of his own," says Mitchell. "You look at his size, his stroke . . . . But Doc is so nice. He'll come inside on you, but never too far. Never. Yet if the hook is working, you've got no chance. God couldn't hit him then."

This softness in Gooden is surrounded by an iron constitution. Except for his stay at Smithers, Gooden has never missed a start because of injury, illness, or hangover, and he has never used so much as a cube of ice on his arm. Through Sunday he had started 142 big league games and completed 49 of them. Gooden's motion is so fluid that it's one of the reasons he has never been good at holding base runners on. The jerky motion of the pickoff is anathema to him.

When Doc was nineteen, he was a 190-pound flamethrower. Now he's a 210-pound metronome of consistency. "You see him, you have to think about a Tom Seaver or a Nolan Ryan," says Mets pitching coach Mel Stottlemyre. "I don't know if anyone can throw as hard as Nolan for as long as Nolan has. But if anybody can do it, I think it will be Dwight."

On May 20, Gooden missed inside and hit Dodgers short-stop Alfredo Griffin on the right hand, breaking it. Afterward, Gooden stood impassively on the mound. "I was thinking, How did I hit him? How did I miss that much?" he says. "I heard he later said I tried to [hit him intentionally]. But I've never thrown at anybody in my life. I don't need to do that. That's not pitching. When I say that I pitch in and out, up and in, I don't mean the same things as other guys. They think, If a guy hits you, come back and hit him. But to me that doesn't make sense. That's not baseball."

Gooden spends hours studying the box scores and the scouting reports. "Usually, I want to run it away from righthanders and in on lefthanders," he says. "I get more ground balls that way. The curve, the change, they set up the fastball. The fastball is my pitch. I study because I'm not going to let certain guys beat me. I don't care if I have to walk a Mike Schmidt, a Dale Murphy, an Andres Galarraga four times a game. They're not going to beat me if I can help it."

Gooden is third on the Mets' alltime winning list, with 84, behind Tom Seaver (198) and Jerry Koosman (140). He's also the youngest player ever to have won the Cy Young Award and to have played in the All-Star Game. His earned run average this season after his 7-2 victory against the Houston Astros on Saturday was 2.90, which seems high only because Gooden had a 2.46 lifetime ERA going into this year. His 11-4 record seems unremarkable because his lifetime winning percentage is .735. Whitey Ford's was .690; Christy Mathewson's, .665; Cy Young's, .620; Bob Gibson's, .591. Last season, even though Gooden didn't start pitching until June, he tied for fifth in the Cy Young vote with Ryan, who, incidentally, is a .517 pitcher over his career.

"That travesty he went through [his drug rehabilitation] helped him," says Carter. "He turned a negative into a plus. I didn't say turning. I mean he's already done it. His marriage seemed to stabilize him."

It seems ironic that a pitcher with Gooden's control would need stabilizing. But his erratic behavior first manifested itself on the mound. As 1986 drew to a close, he was not the same pitcher he had been, even though he finished with a 17-6 record and a 2.84 ERA. He was laboring, and the fastball was not his best pitch anymore. In the National League Championship Series against the Astros, Gooden pitched 17 innings with an ERA of 1.06, but was 0-1. Then, in the World Series, he was shelled by the Boston Red Sox: 0-2 with an 8.00 ERA. Those statistics indicated that something was wrong with Doc.

On October 28, Gooden, apparently suffering from a hang-over, missed the victory parade up Broadway for the world-champion Mets. Two months later came the famous set-to with the Tampa police following an incident involving an alleged traffic violation. The man who had always avoided being hit was caught in a sequence of hits. One of them featured Carlene Pearson, Gooden's former girlfriend, who, while on her way to the gate to meet Doc when he arrived at New York's La Guardia Airport on January 30, was arrested for trying to get through the metal detector with a loaded derringer. "I had hit rock bottom," says Gooden now. "I was in no-man's-land. I just wanted to run, leave, get away. Those were tough times."

Straw knew Doc was too accommodating to his old acquaintances in Tampa. "He's got to get out of there," Straw told reporters at the time. Gooden's high school coach, Billy Reed, a Tampa native, said the same thing. But Doc just couldn't hurt people he knew—even if they were hurting him. So he volunteered for a drug test in March 1987, tested positive for cocaine, took the rap, and let circumstances distance him from those who didn't mean him well. "The hardest thing I've ever done in my life was facing my folks and telling them about the cocaine," Gooden says. "My little boy was there, too. Sitting right there, listening to me."

Reporters shouted questions and cameras whined as Gooden checked into the Smithers clinic on April 2. "Even later during my stay, it was like that," Gooden says. "I'd go to the kitchen to get something to eat, look out the window and there would be reporters and cameramen."

"He wanted to get better," says Dr. Alan Lans, Gooden's counselor and an associate director at Smithers. "This is never easy. Do you have any bad habits? You ever try to quit a habit?

It takes concentration, hard work. But he's getting better all the time."

After he left the clinic, Gooden gave up on his hometown. He bought a house in nearby St. Petersburg for his parents, one he can also use occasionally in the off-season. But New York is home now. "I know I said I thought about giving up the game, but I didn't say that right," says Gooden. "That's not what I meant. I love baseball, and I didn't realize how much until I was away from it. Everything in baseball is familiar to me. It's who I am."

Monica Colleen Harris (who's three years younger than Gooden) and Doc were friends from childhood. She is the sister of Randy and Randall Harris, who played with and against Gooden in high school. "They used to say, 'Don't be looking over there,' but they were laughing," says Gooden. "Besides, she was so young." But even as he began to hit bottom, he noticed her through the haze. She worked the drive-in window at a local Burger King. Doc found himself heading for Burger King often. Then he told one of his relatives to get her phone number. When Gooden was released from Smithers, he called Monica right away. The two were married in Tampa on November 21. It seemed like a whirlwind courtship, but it was an old relationship that had merely changed. It was a fastball set up by a curve.

"It means something to have a nice meal waiting for you," says Gooden. "To have someone to listen and understand what you mean. To leave the game at the park. She doesn't press me to go out. She lets me call the shots."

"When he was striking out sixteen batters a game, he was just throwing," says Johnson. "Now he's a little bigger, happier, more mature. And he'll just go on from here."

"All this stuff made me a better person," says Gooden. "It showed me how much I care about the game of baseball." Yes, soft is the wrong word for Doc. Yet there it is.

When Mets general manager Frank Cashen is asked if he would ever let Straw or Doc go, he mulls the question over only briefly. "I have no present intent to do so," says Cashen. "But Mr. Darling, Mr. Cone, and Mr. Myers have to be signed. It's not an easy set of circumstances."

Strawberry's contract runs until the end of next season, when he'll be eligible to become a free agent. Gooden's contract is up this year, when he'll be eligible for arbitration. "With the numbers we're about to throw up there, there won't be any question [that the Mets will sign us]," says Strawberry. "You have to believe in yourself before anybody else will. And I know I'm going to get mine."

And Gooden? "I think we're one of the best teams," he says. But is he the best pitcher? Doc drops his head and smiles as if he's embarrassed. The voice goes soft. "When I'm down off the mound, I can't answer that," he says. "When I'm on the mound, out there by myself, I feel there is no better pitcher. I don't put anybody before me. I think I'm the best at it. But you can't always win."

Losing is part of growing up. Even the best baseball club on the planet will win a third and lose a third of its games, just like the worst club. It's the other third that makes the difference. Straw and Doc have always had great futures. But now that they also have pasts, those futures may finally be within their reach.

—*Sports Illustrated, July 11, 1988*

TYSON

The following essay was originally written as a letter to Wiley's son, Cole, in his 1989 boxing memoir, Serenity. *The nineteen-year-old Mike Tyson who Wiley first encountered in the Catskills was not yet the heavyweight champion, but even then he could see it was only a matter of time. And in one prescient exchange, Wiley also warned the young fighter to keep his guard up outside the ring: "You owe it to yourself, Mike. Just be careful. You can beat anybody, but you have to be careful."*

I met Mike Tyson on May 5, 1986, in Glens Falls, New York, the day before he was to fight James "Quick" Tillis. A press conference was called at a local hotel. Mike came in and was surrounded. I had to convince myself that this was a nineteen-year-old. He looked like two nineteen-year-olds. His legs were thick pillars of muscle, slabs merely hinged by knees. His neck size had been reported at nineteen inches, and after standing next to him, I considered this a low estimate. It would take a Liston or a Foreman or a baseball bat to hurt this kid. His chin was a long, even horizon. His jawline ridged out from his neck. He had puncher's hands—his fingers were short and thick, his palms immense. I looked him in the eye. He nodded with interest.

I caught him later in the hotel hallway, after he had done a five-minute sit-down television interview. He was agreeable and courteous. I was as impressed with his bearing and his way of expressing himself as with his battleship physique. He was skilled at talking with the media, honest while he was playing its game. He was no politician.

"You handle yourself pretty well, Mike. It's all up front with you. And I haven't even seen you fight yet."

"Oh, he said, in that impossibly light voice, "You'll like me in there. I go about my business."

I asked him to make a fist. He did. It looked like he already had a glove on. He had nearly a flat plane on the knuckle side, the business end of his hand. He was about five-foot-ten, I'd say. He weighed 215 pounds. He bulged all over the place, and where he didn't bulge, he was hard and even and flat. And he just had this look: this Geech look; this Lew Jenkins look; this Tommy look. The look of iron. The lisping voice only barely made him seem less ominous.

George Plimpton once wrote that he had thought being knocked out by Archie Moore in the ring would not be unlike "being tucked in by a Haitian mammy." As I stood there nose to nose with this nineteen-year-old engine of destruction, I thought that being knocked out by Iron Mike Tyson would be like being tucked in by God. Tyson's presence was completely suited to his business, more so than that of any other fighter I had seen since Duran—more so than Duran's, more so than Hearns's, far more so than a Leonard's or Ali's or Hagler's. Tyson seemed just as pitiless as Duran or Hearns, and Tyson weighed 215.

Yet he could be a sweet kid. He happened to grow up tough, in the bloodhole bowels of Brooklyn, and just happened to hit harder than winter at the South Pole. He was living in the Catskills. It was driving him crazy, socially, which is why he had looked at me with interest at the press conference. We were the only black men there. His solitude was all for the best for his fighting at this point. He was at the stage where it was not a question of succeeding, it was a question of avoiding failure.

"I've been trying to get next to some girls," he said.

"You owe it to yourself, Mike. Just be careful. You can beat anybody, but you have to be careful."

"Maybe in a year I could beat anybody," he said. "I don't know if I could beat anybody now."

As we stood talking, I spread my feet apart in order to meet him eye to eye better, as I was a couple of inches taller. I don't know, maybe this was some ritualistic stance from the streets of New York, something of which I knew nothing about, like the hand in the jacket pocket of my youthful days. Tyson, laughing, said, "Lookit you. What you wanna do? You wanna do something? You stand there like that against me? Where you from, the Bronx?"

He squared off, smiling. I laughed and said, "No" as many times as I could in ten seconds. I was not from the Bronx, as was Mitchell Green, Tyson's intended opponent after Tillis. "So, Mike, you'll square anybody off, right?"

"Right. But people started squaring me off first. I got beat up a few times. I didn't like it."

Tyson could have used a father or an uncle or someone else to be a confidant, not merely on boxing but on all matters pertaining to manhood. His manager was Jimmy Jacobs, whom I respected because of his vast knowledge of the sport. But Tyson needed a friend, a mentor, not as Cus D'Amato had been or as Jacobs was. In the end, he was a meal ticket to them. Nobody understood this better than Tyson. "I fight whoever my manager wants me to fight. I'm just a fighter."

It seemed odd to me that a fighter like Tyson, who would have to be close to do damage, would be asked to tie up his greatest protection—the power of his punches—by inverting his hands and holding them in front of his face à la Floyd Patterson, in D'Amato's desired peekaboo stance. This might have been fine for Patterson in 1961. But Tyson was a different kind of fighter entirely. His success depended on hitting the other guy harder than the other guy could hit him. His dimensions were those of a great fighter, not of a classic boxer, a defender. Perhaps he could become a great boxer, one day. But he was already a great fighter in 1986.

Saturday was the day of the fight. As the crowd began to assemble at the Glens Falls Civic Arena for the fight, a half-naked Tyson came out of his dressing room to take a look at the house. He wore his trademark black trunks and black shoes without socks. An adoring public immediately piled in around him, asking for recognition in the form of autographs.

Do something with your hands for me, Mike. Tyson signed, then moved back toward the dressing room. His companion, a young white man, said to him, "Do you believe the nerve of white people?" Tyson laughed at this double talk.

A few minutes later, the nineteen-year-old manchild snorted in disgust and stepped back to compose himself. This was an unusual posture for Tyson. He had never taken a backward step in a procedure boxing ring before, but now he did. He had moved up in fighting class, and it showed. Sooner or later, boys will be boys. Even if they are undefeated.

Tillis had befuddled Tyson by tying up his insistent hammers for the better part of four rounds. This sudden indecision on Tyson's part was Tillis's best chance to shake up the boxing world. He threw caution to the winds and launched his best left hook, intending to circle Tyson's peekaboo defense. Tillis's left hook missed. Tyson, finally presented with the bull's-eye, fired a short left hook in return. It was not his best punch—not even close—but it landed clearly on Tillis's jaw. Tillis's eyes rolled up in his head as he went sprawling toward the canvas, a victim of Tyson's Complaint with thirteen seconds left in round four.

Tillis wasn't saved by the bell, but he was grateful for it. Once the bell stopped ringing in his head, he'd get back where he belonged. On his bicycle. He'd teach this ferocious kid how to survive in the ring. Let somebody else suffer the consequences of trading haymakers with Mike Tyson. "I've heard of baby-sitting," Tillis would say later, "but this is ridiculous."

Tillis's manager, Beau Williford, had said, "It's tough to hit shadows," just before the fight, and with that knockdown as warning, Quick went back to ducking Tyson's bombs and occasionally punching out smart combinations. At times Tillis made Tyson look young, unfinished, but mainly, Tillis merely survived. He lost a ten-round unanimous decision as Tyson won his twentieth straight pro fight. The bloodied Tillis was the first man to go the distance with the manchild. Maybe that would be worth an asterisk one day.

"He punched harder than the Acorn, Earnie Shavers," Tillis said while Tyson entered the interview area. Tillis then said, "Boy, you punch harder than a muthafucka."

Tyson accepted the sincere compliment with a knitted brow. He was not in a particularly good mood, though he'd handled a twenty-seven-year-old contender with relative ease. The trouble with being Mike Tyson will always be that he can never knock his opponents out soon enough. The crowd always wants more of that. The world looked at his 215 sculpted pounds, his ominous glower, his wrecking-ball punches, and said, "That's my champion. Show 'em, Mike."

Boxing is not that easy. "Some people want to rush Mike," Jimmy Jacobs said. "The object isn't for him to fight for the heavyweight championship. The object is for him to win the world championship."

After Tyson had won his last fight, a third-round knockout

over Steve Zouski, in Uniondale, New York, on March 10, he had felt he had to apologize to everybody for not dispatching Zouski in a more expeditious fashion. "I'm having personal problems," Tyson said achingly. Tyson was still a nineteen-year-old, and as such, yearned for the joys of youth, joys which are usually denied a working heavyweight contender. "Girlfriend problems" was how his co-manager Bill Cayton portrayed Tyson's lament. It seems Tyson, ever honest, did go a little stir-crazy up in the Catskills, with nobody around to keep him company other than trainer Kevin Rooney, "stepmother" Camille Ewald, a few pet pigeons (Where that idea came from, I never knew, but I wrote it off to Budd Schulberg and *On the Waterfront*), and some unfortunate sparring partners. "Hey, I was running around looking for girls," Tyson had said, "But I had to decide, did I want to hang out at night, did I want to be a playboy? I didn't."

That, of course, was on a day-to-day basis, and never written in stone. Tyson suffered an ear injury when he fell while trying to capture a rogue pigeon. His left ear swelled to three times its normal size after the fight with Zouski. Treatment at Mount Sinai hospital brought him back to New York, where you never knew how people might be standing. Rooney, in the Catskills, became frantic. Cayton insisted both he and Jacobs knew about the trip. There was also a little ruckus at the Crossgates Mall in Albany. One of Mike's friends threw some sweaters around. Ordinary stuff, until the next champion is involved. Tyson was at the Tryon School for Boys at the age of thirteen. To think that he would reach thirty without any kind of newsworthy public behavior was ludicrous. If Mike Tyson had acted like Sean Penn in public, four or five people would have been dead by then.

Tyson took his frustrations out on the sparring partners before the Tillis fight. Tyson hit one with what Rooney described as "the perfect uppercut," loosening four of the poor man's teeth. Another sparring partner was knocked down on his first two days at the job. "I told Mike to stop hittin' him after a while," said Rooney. "I ain't no butcher." Another sparring partner, looking to mix it up, was knocked cold. Tyson wore eighteen-ounce gloves during all these sessions. Even pillows couldn't muffle the thunder.

"Sooner or later, somebody has to try hitting Mike on the chin," said heavyweight James Broad, who attended the Tillis fight and saw Tillis try it. Back to the drawing board. His best right hands bounced harmlessly off Tyson's jaw.

"Tillis ran, just like we knew he would," said Tyson. "And anybody can look good running. But nobody will beat me by running. Nobody." With that, Tyson rose to leave, and nobody had to ask where he was headed.

I'll tell you this right now, always take the boxer over the puncher, everything else being equal. With Mike Tyson, everything else was not equal. As he continued to fight he amassed all the heavyweight titles, and he also proved to be a difficult riddle to fight. It was amazing how quickly he warmed to the more subtle skills of the professional fighter. He slipped punches with aplomb and had no problems with some of the less than decorous behaviors of in-fighting. Good old Trevor Berbick, our old friend, was stripped of his WBA crown when Tyson knocked him down three times with one punch. One of those you'd have to see to believe. Then Mike dispatched big Pinklon Thomas in Las Vegas. I caught that one live.

Mike was twenty-one by that summer of 1987. He wore a three-day growth of beard before the Thomas fight. He was anxious to get it done and get on with the good stuff about being the champ. I sat down with him at the podium in the Vegas Hilton, and he had no trouble remembering me.

"Yo, main, whatup? How come you couldn't get me on the cover last time?"

"You didn't hurt anybody bad enough, Mike."

"You here with a fighter?"

I looked out over the audience of perhaps two hundred. I saw Earnie Shavers out there, his bald head gleaming magnificently, looking at Mike and smiling.

"I'm here with you, big guy."

"Good selection."

I always enjoyed hearing Tyson describe his fights in that elfin voice. "I threw punches with bad intentions . . . . I was trying to hit him behind the ear . . . in a vital area . . . . It was a clean, devastating shot . . . . I'm the baddest man on the planet." After he knocked out Pinklon, "Did you see that hook? Ooo, that was nice. That took all the fight right out of him." This kind of elocution made Tyson unique. He dissected himself and what he was doing in a cold, almost clinical fashion. He could say what he wanted to do to you. He knew why.

This was chilling to some people who considered the harmless patter of Muhammad Ali threatening. Ali was having fun most of the time, warming to the lights of the stage, making love to the camera, or merely defending himself. Tyson knew he was no television personality. What he could do was the thing. He could hit you harder than you could hit him. There was no doubt that he was more intelligent than Ali, to me. Ali had been quick with repartee, witty in his way, but Tyson seemed to me to be much more reflective, much more volatile. He knew what was happening to him. He just didn't have enough experience to make sense of it, but he knew, even as it all happened. He reminded me of my old friend, the Geechie.

Before the Thomas fight, I visited Pinklon's suite, where the contender, former heroin addict and part-time singer, was busy trying to develop a keen distaste for Tyson.

"He told me to suck his dick!" Pink said incredulously.

This was an insult which left Pink with no alternative but to fight as he had never fought before. If the guy in Philadelphia had told me that, we'd still be there today. So Tyson had tried to make it easier for Pink to stand there and fight him! Some people were casting aspersions on Tyson's sexuality. Fighters usually called each other homosexual, *maricon*. Everyday Joes said this about Mike. One sportswriter for a Los Angeles-area newspaper, Rick Talley, said, "Boxing has come to this. One guy's named Pink, and the other one's a fag," just before the bell rang for the Thomas-Tyson bout.

Nobody said this to Tyson's face, you can be sure. Tyson would hug and kiss his foes after he had blasted them to the deck and they had been revived. He'd kiss Rooney on the mouth in the corner between rounds from time to time. Far from making him suspect, I figured this only made Tyson all the more secure. He'd kiss whoever he felt like kissing. Word was going around that Tyson was taking girls out of clubs three at a time, now that they were readily available to him. Tyson was always aware of the manner in which he was perceived. He seemed well able to dismiss it, telling one television interviewer, "Look, so I'm supposed to be homosexual or I'm supposed to be taking all these women out of nightclubs." Then he merely shrugged, as if to say, "Make of it what you will."

Before Pink was KO'd, one of his manager-backers said to me, "I think it's gonna take an Ali type to beat this Tyson guy. That's what I think. This guy hits like nobody else."

Hardly. Tyson hit rather like Sonny Liston, rather like George Foreman. In fact, in fights involving the three of them, I rather thought George might have the edge in punching power. While it was true that Ali had taken the measure of

Liston and Foreman, there were no more Alis. Ali was not a type. If the world had to wait for an Ali type to beat Mike Tyson, the world would be waiting awhile.

After dispatching Pinklon, Tyson was charged with assault and battery with deadly weapons in Los Angeles after taking a parking attendant to task with but the heel of his palm after Mike had ogled and asked for a kiss from a female parking attendant. This is a good lesson, son. Never stand between the heavyweight champion and his chosen. Tyson ran around after Tony Tucker, who was 35-0 and a boxer type. He hit Tyson in the first round with a great left uppercut that (physically) lifted Tyson up and knocked him back six inches. The point here, though, was that the punch didn't even daze Tyson. It had no effect on his clarity of thought, even though it knocked him back. Tyson had something unique—that buttressing neck. That neck and chin combined as an impregnable defense. "After he hit me, it was history," Tyson said. "It just went away."

Tyson hit hard, but no harder than Liston or Foreman or Joe Louis. The most devastating quality was the speed of his punches. He got off quicker than any heavyweight since Louis, as far as the power punchers go. At times he seemed to be as quick as Ali. Some people tried to compare Tyson to Joe Frazier, but there was no comparison to be made. Tyson was far superior to Frazier. The only person even close to the image of an Ali type during this time was Michael Spinks, who had held up well. Michael had all the experience Tyson lacked. Spinks had fought against Mustafa, against Indian Yaqui, against Holmes, thirty rounds' worth. And in taking the title from Holmes, Spinks could lay claim to the heavyweight title— only until he met Tyson. Always take the boxer over the puncher, son, everything else being equal. Spinks had the experience to make it interesting, to lead on points briefly, perhaps. But he was flatly outgunned, outweighed, overmatched. When Ali had beaten Liston and Foreman, he had backed them up, knocked them out. He was as big as they were. Unless Spinks could do that to Tyson, he would have no chance. But it might be worth the price of admission.

It was this linkage to the puncher, to Liston and Foreman and Frazier and Marciano and Louis and Dempsey and Johnson, that gave Tyson his mystique and his great advantage in three Ali-less years. This is what made old George Foreman mount a comeback in 1987—the thought of Tyson. This is what brought Earnie Shavers to Las Vegas. Tyson spoke a language they understood. They *knew* Tyson. They *were* Tyson. Tyson walked past Earnie in the Hilton ballroom. Earnie giggled and asked for a shot. Mike clapped him on his shoulder. Hard. Just so Earnie would know he was not to be played with. And Earnie understood him. *Everybody* understood him, somehow. It was as Lew Jenkins had said. You can win a certain way and nobody cares. But that hot rod!

After Tyson manhandled Pinklon, he strode through the Las

Vegas Hilton with a security guard on each side of him. The guards were window dressing, superfluous. The lobby of the Hilton was crammed full of people. They parted before Tyson, fell back in awe as he strode through, rolling his shoulders, walking as if he owned the joint, which he surely did. I walked behind him in his wake, watching the faces of humanity as their prizefighting champion came within arm's length of them. Everybody understood Mike Tyson.

But for every bull there is a matador. It's a matter of putting the right two together. So, all things equal, always take the boxer over the puncher—unless the puncher was Mike Tyson when you were a little boy.

Tyson had no idea of how to properly court Robin Givens. He just waded in throwing. He visited her apartment in the wee hours of the morning just to ask her to be his girlfriend, and the first time he tried to kiss her, she ran. As a tactician, if indeed these were tactics, Robin Givens was Leonardesque. Tyson only knew he had been smitten by her. He found himself outside her apartment ringing her doorbell, not taking her initial no for an answer. No was not an answer suitable for the heavyweight champion of the world.

Givens and Tyson had a whirlwind courtship which ended in marriage in February 1988, one month before Jimmy Jacobs died and four months before Tyson was to meet Michael Spinks in the largest-grossing athletic event of all time, to be held at the Atlantic City convention hall in June 1988.

Tyson's take was to be between $21 and $22 million for this fight. But he was managed in the old, pre-Ali style. He was giving up thirty-three percent to Bill Cayton and Jimmy Jacobs's widow. Robin Givens had already surmised this after there was a delay when she and Tyson decided to buy a $4.5 million house in New Jersey. Entertainers are accustomed to their agents' getting anywhere from three to five percent, and ten percent is around normal for other professionals. Robin Givens could count. She had dated Eddie Murphy and Michael Jordan before she met Tyson, and those who think that Tyson's pre-Spinks net value in the neighborhood of $50 million had something to do with her interest in him are not being naive. Of course it did. Probably no one knew this better than Tyson. He was too smart not to know.

But the spell of the heavyweight champion of the world is quite enough to woo most women, no matter how much hard business is involved. After Tyson performed the inevitable knockout of Spinks, Robin sat on Tyson's right, holding his right hand—the same right that had just dispatched Spinks—while Tyson addressed the media. Robin rubbed his hand against her cheek and closed her eyes. A relationship between a man and a woman is based as much on security as on love, and Robin Givens knew in her soul that for all Tyson was not, he in fact made her the most secure woman in the world. She was rich, and she had the ultimate protector. I believed this was more than even she had bargained for.

Shortly after this, Tyson took on the real estate magnate Donald Trump as an adviser, and sued for separation from Cayton. Jack Dempsey had done almost precisely the same thing sixty years earlier, marrying a Hollywood starlet, fighting in Atlantic City, separating himself from his managers at his wife's insistence. Yet Tyson was castigated from pillar to post in the media, and, of course, this was racist at its core.

Of his $21 million purse for Spinks, Cayton's cut was $7 million. Even Rooney, a mere trainer, got $2.1 million, ten percent, and expenses. All this before the Internal Revenue Service came to call. Of course, this was ridiculous to Robin Givens. It would be ridiculous to anyone not used to the involuntary servitude of black people. Cayton was just a wallet. Tyson was just a fighter. Other words were pressed into service in the media, like "caring," "loyalty," "disbelief," "ingratitude," and plenty of gossip about Robin Givens. Tyson was said to have beaten her. She appeared constantly and was always unmarked. And it would have been worse, but the bottom line was that Robin Givens was Tyson's wife.

One writer in a New York newspaper went so far as to write an open letter to Tyson, saying in it, "I don't care about your wife." Between the lines was, "I care about Bill Cayton." But with Robin Givens in the equation, the issue could not be so cut-and-dried. *Sharecropper getting uppity* wouldn't fly in the face of the holy institution of matrimony. Marriage meant turning over that institution, superseding it for the invisible institution of racism. It had to die down, or at least become more subtle. Soon after the fight, Cayton settled out of court for something like 16 percent—still quite a chunk of change for what had been maybe a $100,000 investment, total, in the beginning. Robin Givens had performed her service for Tyson. And he had performed his service for her. It was a fair exchange for the time being.

In August 1988, the undefeated heavyweight champion of the world got into a street fight with Mitchell Green, whom Tyson had already decisioned in the ring more than a year earlier. Green was a former street gang leader who hadn't had a ring fight since Tyson had whipped him. The only reasons he had survived then were a pair of good legs and an ability to cover up. I don't know, perhaps the fact that he had gone the distance with Tyson gave him a kind of honor. "I fought Mike Tyson, and he didn't knock me out."

So Mitchell Green and Mike Tyson took it to the street. They were on the one-two-five, 125th Street in Harlem, in front of Dapper Dan's, a haberdashery and house of games with a bit of a reputation for nefarious late-night activities. Above the haberdashery was a window painted with the words DOCTOR OFFICE. There were two versions of the story about that night. Green said Tyson started it. Tyson said Green started it. In any event, Tyson ended it. Green did admit he called Tyson a sissy. If he did this to Tyson's face, I have no doubt who started it.

Green was a big man, well over six feet, around 240 pounds

at the time of this smoker. Tyson only hit him once, with a right to his face. Tyson's hand was not in a glove, but his fist was so solid and thick it still would take tremendous pressure for him to break his hand, which he did—a hairline fracture of the third metacarpal. Green was not so lucky. He needed five stitches in his nose and suffered a black eye.

Walter Berry, a professional basketball player, and a relative of his, Thomas Smalls, were in Tyson's company that night. Tyson could afford better company, but he chose not to do so. Who knows if this was guilt or desire for a kind of acceptance he would never know downtown? Tyson likes the word "pure." On the streets, the admiration for what he could do, who he was, was pure. He was a bad motherfucker there. Not a meal ticket or husband or criminal element of an underclass. In the street he was pure, the "baddest man on the planet," in his words. The streets were his mother's milk. No man wants to give that up, no matter what he grows to be.

Shortly after the set-to with Green, Tyson suffered a head injury, was in fact knocked out for nearly an hour and suffered resulting amnesia, after spinning a BMW into a tree by the driveway of Camille Ewald in Catskill, New York. So that's what it would take to knock him out. A car wreck. Doctors reported neurological damage, and Tyson's scheduled fight with a now greatly relieved black man from Britain named Frank Bruno was temporarily canceled.

One story had it that Tyson had attempted suicide this way,

in order to get the attention of Robin Givens. Poppycock. If Tyson wanted to commit suicide, all he needed to do was drop his hands in the ring while fighting. Briefly, I wondered if Tyson, once recovered, would regard this wreck as a kind of sign. He must have been backing out of that driveway at a high speed to have been so injured. He had been in a hurry to move, for some reason. Perhaps this accident was some fate telling him to slow down, to be more careful, to take his time, to be more serene.

If nothing else, the accident proved to him that he could be knocked out. I have always been of the opinion that a fighter does not truly know the totality of fighting until he has been knocked out, technically or otherwise. Now Tyson knew how it felt and in so knowing would probably take pains to see that it didn't happen again soon.

There was no doubt that he was the most fascinating heavyweight champion since Ali. Perhaps Tyson would be the last of the great heavyweight champions before he was through. First, though, he must find peace of mind. The only certainty was that some day he would be through. There were many fights to be fought in the meantime, and only a few of them would occur in the ring. Only time would tell, and time is a bad motherfucker.

The other silver slipper finally dropped on Friday, October 7, 1988, at approximately 11 a.m., when palimony attorney Marvin Mitchelson file a petition for divorce in the name of Robin Simone Givens, with declarations by Givens, her mother, Ruth Roper, and a family employee, Olga Rosario, in the Los

Angeles Superior Court. Included in this action was a tempo-rary restraining order against Tyson. Tyson then retained Howard Weitzman, formerly the legal counsel for ex-automo-bile tycoon and accused cocaine trafficker John DeLorean, to defend him against Givens's claim of community property under California law. Community property would mean a hail-storm of silver slippers. To her credit, Robin Givens always did say she came in a package deal.

So in the end it was Givens who proved to the world that Tyson could be whipped after all. Seven days before the peti-tion was filed, Givens held an astonishing interview with Barbara Walters on the September 30 edition of ABC-TV's *20/20*, declaring that "Michael is a manic-depressive," and that their life together had been "pure hell." Givens outlined an amazing scenario of her fears of Tyson, while Tyson, amaz-ingly self-contained for such an alleged brute, sat and rubbed her back. Later, Tyson admitted he was on drugs at the time, drugs prescribed by doctors Givens had hired. The drugs included some combination of lithium, ativan, desipramine, and thorazine.

Walters: "There was no prenuptial agreement?"

Givens: "No. And why should there be? We got married to be together, not to plan for divorce . . . . I want to live with Mike for the rest of my life, and I want to have little Tysons . . . . that can't happen if Michael doesn't get help."

Tyson: "If you are going to marry somebody, you trust them.

My wife just has to ask for it and she has everything I have. If she wants to right now, take—she can leave right now, take everything I have and just leave."

Givens: "Just recently I've become afraid. I mean very much afraid . . . . Michael is a manic-depressive. He is . . . ."

Hardly. Tyson was diagnosed by one Dr. Henry McCurtis as a manic-depressive shortly after the car accident. He was taking lithium, ativan, and desipramine by the time he accompanied Givens and Roper and a female "former employee" of Givens to Moscow, along with Rosario, where Givens was filming a segment of the television show, *Head of the Class.*

According to the declarations of Givens, Roper, and Rosario, Tyson drank heavily while in Moscow, then broke champagne bottles and threatened and chased Ruth and Robin around the hotel. The one certainty was that Tyson never felt he needed to take drugs. He was trying to please his wife, but something was wrong and he knew it instinctively. A Dr. Abraham Halpern, who was hired by Bill Cayton, claimed Tyson was not a manic-depressive after an hour-long consultation with Tyson at Cayton's office. "I don't know the details of his sexual life," said Dr. Halpern, "but there's no doubt that that's part of the problem here."

Givens: "When he's in a depressive state he doesn't sleep. He has enormous amounts of energy. So your sleeping agitates him. He gets you up. There's an argument. I mean, of course you want to sleep."

"I saw nothing that would support a diagnosis of manic depression or psychosis," said Dr. Halpern. The seven symptoms of manic depression are as follows: inflated self-esteem, decreased need for sleep, more talkative than usual, flights of ideas, distractibility, increase in goal-directed activity, and excessive involvement with pleasurable activities. By those criteria, half the people in New York City could be diagnosed manic-depressive. In fact, those symptoms and others that Tyson manifested—threats, call after call to Givens when they were apart, fits of jealousy and name-calling, then cow-eyed acceptance of even the most ridiculous of Given's orders and pronouncements—these were symptomatic of another illness: lovesickness. There is no drug to control that.

On Sunday, October 1, according to the declarations of Rosario, Roper, and Givens, Tyson drank heavily, called Rosario in particular "whore" and "slut," and beat Robin Givens about the face and body at their Bernardsville, New Jersey, mansion on fifteen acres. Givens claimed Tyson hit her with a drinking glass. Just before the local police arrived, Tyson threw an andiron through a foyer window and drove away in his BMW. Givens filed no complaint with the police. "That's not unusual," said Bernardsville police chief Thomas J. Sciaretta. Sciaretta had met Tyson before. "He was always quite calm, and very polite to me. We never had any complaints from neighbors, none at all. I think he thought he could move to Bernardsville and be left alone. It didn't happen for him. It's been like a siege at that house. The man could not come out of his own door without people with microphones and cameras around. I personally ran some of them out. I think that's what happened when he threw a radio at a film crew when he was out running one morning last week. And do you know what? I don't blame him."

Tyson was obsessed with his wife. There was historical precedent. Dempsey left his manager at the behest of a Hollywood wife. Louis was obsessed with Lena Horne after what was only to have been a tryst of mutual admiration. Tyson had never been in league with a woman like Givens before. She introduced him to another world. Many go through this, especially around their early twenties. As it happened, Givens broke Tyson's heart, but at least now he knew he had one. Anything else that got broken was purely optional. Givens made an error in going for the quick knockout. Mitchelson, it turned out, was being represented by Weitzman in an action filed by two of Mitchelson's former clients, who were alleging sexual assault and rape. Givens would immediately drop Mitchelson and hire a New York attorney, Raoul Felder, who said he merely hoped to reach an out-of-court settlement. With all the skeletons rattling around in Givens's closet, and considering the estimable talents of Weitzman, it was no wonder. "Clearly, the personalities involved are interesting," Weitzman said. "There's something here that's not right. I spoke to Mike and his interest is to make sure the proceedings be conducted in a gentlemanly manner. My impression from the get-go is, why was this petition filed in California and not in New Jersey. My improvement is that this is a great relief to Michael. He's disappointed, but his mind is clear." Soon after this, Tyson announced, "Sometimes you have to go beyond love. Sometimes you can love someone who doesn't love you in return." Soon after this, he said, "There's no more turmoil." Tyson was a quick study, keenly intelligent even in the throes of love. In his own brave words, he was "a conscious black man!" And he was still heavyweight champion.

—*From Serenity: A Boxing Memoir, 1989*

RICE IS A BREED APART

Wiley returned to the Bay Area for this 1987 Sports Illustrated *profile of Jerry Rice, who was then in his third season with the San Francisco 49ers. Written as a strategy briefing for the top defenders in the league, Wiley's scouting report informed them what the rest of the NFL would soon learn about the greatest receiver of all time: There is simply no stopping the man known as Fifi.*

O kay, gentlemen, are you all here? Green. Hayes. Irvin. Lewis. Walls. Good, then, let's start the briefing. Put your egos in your watch pockets. We want all you elite cornerbacks to grasp the gravity of the situation. Things are getting out of hand with San Francisco's Jerry Rice. Item: He has three gears—fast, very fast, and gone. Item: He can fake the decals off your helmet without disturbing the paint. Item: At six-foot-two, 200 pounds, he's perfectly built to carry out his missions. We know that most of you like to work one-on-one, but we want you to work closely with your safeties on this operation. All we can do is warn you. Now listen up. We have Rice's voice on tape. Here's what he has to say about each of you:

■ Darrell Green, Redskins. "Vulnerable to the slant shake. He'll bite hard on the slant because he feels he's got the speed to recover. Bite. Shake. Gone!"

■ Lester Hayes, Raiders. "Get him on the third move. Take him in, out, come under. Let him alongside. Nod out, break back hard inside. The opening will be there."

■ LeRoy Irvin, Rams. "The comeback. First thing he'll do is take off. He doesn't want you behind him. So eat up his cushion. Turn him. Once he's turned—once anybody's turned—he's mine."

■ Albert Lewis, Chiefs. "Good speed. Need more than one move. On Albert, I have to run three outs, with an out shake in there. Change the order. Let him decide. As soon as he lifts that foot to turn, shake, burn, by him."

■ Everson Walls, Cowboys. "Ah, Everson. You've got to take him a couple of extra steps into a route. You've got to use your head, your eyes. Be subtle. Out, in, then in hard. Look for the ball to the post. Demand the ball in the post with your eyes. See, you've got to make him believe it. Then shoot to the corner. On Everson, you want to run a go, a burn, and you want to do it early. Then we've got a ball game."

We see we have your attention now, gentlemen. Save your indignation. It won't help you. You're dealing with a cold executioner. You must study Jerry Rice—what he does, when he does it, how he thinks, what he doesn't like. You must find the flaw in his character. You must know him as well as you know yourselves. Why? So you won't embarrass yourselves or the cities and the institutions you represent when Rice comes to terrorize you and tread on your painted end-zone grass. Are you with us now? We thought you might be. By the numbers, then.

1. GETTING OPEN

"I need my space," says Rice. "That's just the way I am. I don't like crowds." He has just eaten dinner in the cafeteria at Sierra College in Rocklin, California, where the 49ers hold their training camp. Rice even looks open in the dinner line. He's part of the group, yet off to one side. Some of the guys may joke with him on certain days, but this isn't one of them. Rice is wearing stone-washed jeans over legs that belong on a horse, dark glasses, and the hairdo that led some teammates to call him Fifi, as in poodle cut. They called him that before he shocked the NFL last season, his second in the league, by scoring 16 touchdowns and catching 86 passes for 1,570 yards. That's the third-highest receiving yardage total in NFL history. The top two—Charley Hennigan's 1,746 yards and Lance Alworth's 1,602—came during the aerial circus that was the AFL.

Twice last year, Rice caught three TD passes in a game. He had 12 receptions for 204 yards against Washington—and dropped three passes. The drops suggest he's human. Ignore that for now. At only twenty-four, Rice is running his name into the record books with a smooth and impeccable stride. "But the number one thing about receiving, getting open, is speed," says Rice. "Speed's essential."

Throw out those 40-yard-dash times, gentlemen. They mean nothing. Nowadays everybody says he runs at least 4.4. Outside of, oh, twenty guys, everybody is lying. "I'm a 4.4," says Rice with a gleam in his eye. Not all the time. The book says he's a 4.6. But it doesn't matter what he runs in shorts for a guy holding a stopwatch. That's track. You don't play track. You run track. You play football. "Jerry's got game speed," says San Francisco safety Ronnie Lott. "He's 4.2 in games. Hard to explain, but nobody outruns Jerry in a game."

"It's the speed coming out of the break, the speed with the uniform on, the speed of the first five steps," says Rice. "My first five steps are right now. I'm on you. Sprinters don't have the full body control you need. They chop their steps going into cuts. I accelerate into my cuts, accelerate again coming out of them. I amaze myself, sometimes."

Rice developed his speed as a kid growing up outside Crawford, Mississippi, which is thirty-eight miles from Starkville, which is where you can get the bus to Jackson. And from Jackson, two or three plane rides will get you almost anywhere. Rice grew up simon-pure. No street lights or sidewalks or traffic sings or stadium concerts. No drugs or crime or sirens. No distractions.

When Rice wanted a good time as a boy, he and some of his five brothers would go into the family's field and chase the neighbors' horses who grazed there. "They didn't just come to you," Rice says. "If you wanted to ride, you chased them down." So the Rice brothers would pursue the horses, zigging and zagging over seven acres of farmland. When they caught the horses, they would ride bareback.

"He just gets . . . so open," 49er quarterback Joe Montana says of Rice. "He has the knack of knowing when to break, when to use his speed." Backup quarterback Steve Young says, "What makes Jerry so special is his body language. I've never seen anything like it, what he can do to a defensive back. Yet at the same time, the quarterback can read him perfectly. Whenever he has an optional cut, it's like, I know where he's going to go."

The reason Rice gets so open is that defensive backs have so much trouble figuring out where he's going to go. In an August 15, preseason game against the Raiders, Rice sold cornerback Lionel Washington on the post and then beat him to the corner and caught a 23-yard scoring pass from Young. Piece of cake. Rice beat Washington by five yards. This, gentlemen, was a mismatch. Nothing against Washington, of course, but he has only one pair of legs.

Without Rice, who was sidelined by a broken finger he sustained while blocking in practice, the Niners looked punchless in an August 22, exhibition against the Cowboys. While Rice watched the 13-3 loss from the stands, his body twitched as he vicariously ran patterns against Walls, who intercepted two passes. "I was running and moving," said Rice after the game. "I was yelling, 'You've got to turn him!' My wife, Jackie, thinks I'm crazy."

Rice can get open in his sleep. He'll sometimes break into a pattern in the middle of the night, shaking out of bed in his Redwood Shores townhouse with a jab step, either way, eating up the cushion between him and the bedroom wall. Jackie, who three-and-a-half months ago gave birth to their first child, a daughter named Jaqui, might peer at him and mumble something about there being two babies in the house.

2. ATTITUDE

But we all know that fancy-pants wide receivers who think getting open is the whole show can get their comeuppance. Last January against the Giants, Rice was behind the defense, preparing to take in a Montana pass and score the first touchdown of the NFC semifinal game, when he dropped the ball. "It just came out," says Rice. New York went on to win 42-3. If Rice had held on to that pass, the score probably would've been 42-10. Safety Kenny Hill of the Giants was later fined $5,000 by the NFL for two flagrant hits against Rice. Throughout the game, usually when Rice had his head turned toward a play unfolding on the other side of the field, Hill leveled him with a succession of forearms. Niner coach Bill Walsh demanded punitive action. Rice never uttered a word. "You won't hear me say anything about that, ever, because football is a physical game," says Rice.

The day after San Francisco's loss to the Giants, he began working out. If anything, Rice practices harder than he plays. "He's always at top speed," says Lott. "Young defensive backs want to avoid him in coverage line. Covering Jerry in practice is the closest I'll ever come to covering a Paul Warfield, a Charley Taylor."

"When we went to the Hall of Fame Game, I went in the Hall," says Rice. "It sent chills through me. That's where I want to go. That means this year I'd like to get 90 catches, 18 touchdowns, 1,800 yards [after the 49ers' first two games, a 30-17 loss to Pittsburgh and a 27-26 beating of Cincinnati, in which he grabbed the game-winning TD pass with no time remaining, he was on pace with 12, 3, and 192]. I want to be in there with guys who didn't play for the money as much as for the challenge."

Obviously, we can't wait for Rice to rest on his laurels. We can't count on intimidation. We interrogated Montana further, asking if Rice could still improve. He half smiled, looked away and said, "I don't know if there's anything that he can't already do." So, we've found no physical or attitudinal weakness in Rice. We must probe deeper. Open you red files, gentlemen.

3. DEEP BACKGROUND

Forget those big-school reputations, gentlemen. How many times did Texas or Oklahoma or Alabama throw the ball at you out of a double-split, triple-right, no-huddle offense? Rice helped put Mississippi Valley State in Itta Bena on the map. In one game, he caught 24 passes—and four more were called back by penalties. He went to Valley State because it was the only school that sent a coach to see him.

Before Rice caught the Greyhound to Itta Bena, the Delta

Devils ran a standard pro-set offense. The coach at that time, Archie Cooley, took one look at Rice and began devising all manners of bizarre formations designed to spring Rice loose. Rice caught more than 100 passes in each of his last two seasons. As a senior he had 28 TD receptions. He has faced constant double-teaming since he was an 18-year-old freshman. That's another reason he came so far so fast.

That leaves us with the matter of the dropped passes. It's not a question of hands. Rice's father, Joe, built their house near Crawford with his bare hands. He's a bricklayer whose handiwork can be admired all over Oktibbeha County. Jerry helped his father with his work. He stacked bricks, shoveled and slapped mortar, and banged his knuckles raw. So Jerry's hands are tough. "And he could stand more sun than I could," says Joe. "He handled bricks better than any worker I ever had. I was sorry to see him go."

When Rice chose to play football, his mother, Eddie B., had her doubts. He started out as a skinny boy. "I didn't love it," she says, "but the more I fought it, the more determined he was, so I gave it up." She alludes to Malachi: "You just never know what God has in the storehouse for you."

"It was just fun to them," says Joe. "Tom, Jimmy, and Jerry, they were always after that football. I saw Jerry dive in a thorn bush after a ball one day. He got stuck bad, but he caught it. When I saw that, I felt something." Now Joe will sometimes excuse himself early from church to head back to the house that Jerry bought his parents in Starkville. "I have to come home, just to see my boy on television and get that feeling."

"To tell the truth, I don't know much about it," says Eddie B. "But I have to admit that I like those 49ers now. Before Jerry bought us this house, he said, 'Pick a place.' So we did. Every year, we go to Atlanta to see him play. But Crawford—I liked that little town." Says Jerry, "You know, that's what made me, running those back dirt roads and country fields."

That was then. Nobody can remember Rice ever dropping a pass as a kid. But he dropped two in exhibition games this August. He dropped at least nine last year; if he'd kept that number down, he probably would have broken Hennigan's receiving-yardage record. "I have to clean that up," says Rice.

He's pretty clean, otherwise. Jerry drives a Porsche, and Jackie tools around in a Jag. Jerry owns a Rottweiler named Max, and Jackie has a poodle named Casio. And Jerry is well-dressed. Very GQ. Armani, Ungaro, "whatever looks good," says Jackie. "He's got some clothes; I don't even know what they are," says his father.

So this is all we can give you, gentlemen. Perhaps the dropped balls reflect a tendency to be distracted, to lose his concentration. Maybe the way to cover Rice is to get to know him, be his friend—if you can find the real Rice under the Fifi cut, behind the dark glasses, inside the designer clothes. Turn his head. Tell him how great he is. Maybe he'll believe you.

Maybe he'll forget to catch the ball. We know it isn't much, gentlemen, but it's all we have. You're on your own now. Consider yourselves briefed.

—Sports Illustrated, September 28, 1987

FROM HERE TO INFINITY

In this 2001 GQ *cover story, Wiley profiled Kobe Bryant, who had already won two NBA championships before he was twenty-three. While he concluded that Kobe was only going to get better as a player, Wiley also questioned the young Laker's incredibly private facade (including his months-old marriage) and got him to discuss the high price of fame.*

One great work of art can always help explain others. And so it's no surprise that when Kobe Bryant glides into Jerry's Famous Deli in Marina Del Rey, California, a month removed from helping the Lakers to a second straight NBA title, the framed posters on the walls and ceiling spring into new life, expanded meaning. *A Few Good Men. My One and Only. The Wiz.* Run the offense through Kobe and things get revealed.

"Shaq?" he says, sliding into a booth, scooping up a menu with an average size mitt. (If his paws were as big as Michael's, they'd have to shut down the league.) "Domination! Me? Crazy year. Roller coaster, like Disneyland, Space Mountain, start in darkness, come to light. Me? Just number 8."

"Yeah right," you reply. "Just a number 8 nobody in the world can guard."

Kobe's eyes narrow in amusement, and his laughter is a staccato *rat-tat-tat,* a ghostly reminder of Tupac Shakur. Barely cognizant of his own power, the twenty-three-year-old baller glides into Jerry's Famous smiling but alone—basically alone. No one on his level. Imagine what it feels like. Now multiply that by ten, because he turns out to be more—much more than you can see at a glance. On Kobe's level? Skilled beyond belief, dominant for years to come, New Face of His Sport. Tiger Woods, Kobe Bryant . . . . That's pretty much roll call.

Subplots abound around the Lake's great star who is hard to get to know and is used to being alone. He has alliances, uneasy, new, old, ancient, at times strained. He has ties that bind now and forever. Kobe & Shaq. Kobe & Vanessa Bryant, the New Wife. Kobe & Mom & Dad & Sisters. Kobe & His Few NBA Contempos: Alley I, T-Mac, Vinsanity. Kobe & Phil. Kobe & Buss. Kobe & History. But he is still basically alone. A man can't afford not to see things as they are. Alone. That's how we come here; that's how we leave. In the meantime, we have to work with things as they are and with people as they come. A man, even a flying man, can't afford not to face the gravity of these facts.

"Best on the planet, all nine planets, best in the solar system," said his co-star and occasional foil, the earthshaking seven-one, 335-pound center Shaquille O'Neal, during the Lakers' great blitz through the playoffs, the real season. Once Shaq gave it up to Kobe like that, you knew a war was on. Or over. Shaq and Kobe, same page? Ball game. The Lakers hooped it up big-time, as good as it's ever been done, 15-1 through the postseason, in that league. Whoo!

It was a joyous ending to a volcanic season that once threatened to divide Los Angeles. Kobe got the worst of it. He had to endure threats of a rumored trade. He was called selfish by his own teammates. He was labeled All-Ego by his coach, who told Kobe he had fourteen years to be what he thought he was—what he wanted to be—the world's best baller. Phil Jackson also promoted a scurrilous story that Kobe, while in high school at Lower Merion in Ardmore, Pennsylvania, had "sabotaged" games so he could pull them out in the fourth quarter and look like a hero.

Was there a kernel of truth to Jackson's smear? "Hell no!" says Kobe. "Phil said he wasn't trying to imply anything; he was trying to give somebody an example of my competitive nature. I was like, 'C'mon, Phil.'" Maybe Kobe didn't go to college, but he did score above average on the SAT. "I just filed it. Later on, we were scrimmaging at a practice. Shaq was out with an injury, so it was my team against Horace Grant's team. We were kicking butt, up by like . . . thirty. Phil took me out. I told him, 'Yo, Phil, put me back in there—so I can sabotage us and hit the winning shot.'" Everybody started laughing. Even Phil.

"Truthfully, man, I don't need that kind of motivation. I don't need to be pushed. I'm hungry. We have two NBA titles, two rings, but I'm so hungry for championships it's like we don't have any yet."

Tiger has Jack Nicklaus's eighteen majors. Kobe has Michael's six championships. Russell won eleven. Now, today that would be sick. But that's the measure: championships.

"When I was a young fellow—*heh-heh-heh-heh* I thought they'd just come," says Kid Baller, "along with the rest of it. Now I realize they're the only thing that matters."

There is a perception out there that Kobe Bryant isn't hard, doesn't wear a stocking cap under a baseball cap or a perpetual scowl, talks without using *na'mean* and *knowwhutahmsayin* as commas, can work a room of Joe Nerds wearing pocket protectors as well as he can work the Apollo, goes street or suite, preferably neither, when you get right down to it. Doesn't play Playstation 2 or like to go out we-be-clubbing, won't play cards or whoop it up during warm-ups, none of it. He has bucked the norm since draft day 1996, when he and his dad, Jelly Bean Bryant, turned in early while his fellow draftees partied it up. He's eccentric only according to what is already eccentric. He is what he is because of the way he grew up. Grew up playing alone. Never had to be a teammate like Jordan did at Carolina, never had to fit in with other blue-chippers. He was a high school phenom, had come to that in a solitary fashion, playing by himself for years, in Italy, working on his game, his game being his friend, his escape. He became in this life a loner, in that he knew no one like him, with his set of skills and interests. In high school, the team was totally dependent on him. In order to win, he had to make things happen. He skipped college. He had to learn to trust others in the NBA. Only another ball genius could help him see what he had to do, convince him he'd have to do it, if he wanted to win, *really* win. It wasn't Phil Jackson who helped him see this. It was Jerry West, the old baller genius. Adolph Rupp had once begged West to come to Kentucky, said he was the most amazing thing he'd ever seen on court. West declined, went to West Virginia, then to the NBA. Had his nose broken nine times. Averaged thirty in the playoffs. Nine broken noses. Thirty a game. And won only one NBA title. For a Patrick Ewing, a Charles Barkley, a Pistol Pete Maravich, one NBA title would be a godsend. For a West or a Bryant, one NBA title is only one. There are levels to the game. Kobe Bryant could dig on Jerry West.

"One of my weaknesses had to do with not making my teammates better," Kobe says, in what is undoubtedly music to the ears of all L.A. "Wasn't a conscious effort not to make them better, it was just . . . one of my weaknesses."

Listening to Jerry helped him. Over dinner at Jay-Dub's house, they began to talk, about anything, everything, regular stuff. "After dinner," says Kobe, "we went into his living room and got down to basketball. We talked of the league, the team, myself." No decisions were made that night, but Kobe understood when he left that he had to change, had to reach out. Had to join in the pregame dance-around to fire up the team even if he preferred to focus in solitude. Had to join the card game on the team flight, become one of the fellas, even if he preferred to chill with his CD player and headphones.

"I've always had a different mind-set," he says. "I would try to destroy whomever I was against in practice. Go for the jugular . . . but I realize for the team's sake it's about how many people you elevate."

And so Kobe studied Jerry's example, sorted through his feelings while tapping into Jerry's wisdom. "Jerry is a perfectionist in every sense of the word," he says. "He's really competitive. Told me, 'If I was playing now, I'd kill you, Kobe.'" Does he actually believe it? "Without the shadow of a doubt. Kobe shakes his head in admiration, then laughs his rat-tat-tat laugh. "I tell him, 'Jerry, with all due respect, I'd post your little behind up.'"

"The triangle defense? That was hard to learn," Kobe says, waiting for you to appreciate how rare that is, how private an admission it is for him to say there are things that are hard for him in basketball. "You can never be perfect in the triangle. It's like golf. It's crazy. You take three steps backward to take one forward. After Tiger won the Masters the first time, back in '97, he went through a year where he was struggling because he was trying to refine his stroke. When I was trying to get this triangle down, I went through games where I flat-out got my ass kicked." At the time, Kobe's frustration made it seem as if he wanted to showcase his skills. What he really wanted, craved, was to define himself on a basketball court, much as he'd done his entire life. "It's a process," he explains. "You're in it for the long haul. When you start getting good at it, then you start seeing results. Somebody will be open. The defense chooses who it will be. You adjust your attack to that. Then you start wiping people out."

Drama can be a powerful thing and is not always to be avoided. It can help a professional sports league become ascendant. It can change hearts and minds. So it is a good thing to try to understand. In June's NBA Finals, Kobe almost found himself cast in the role of villain once again. Allen Iverson, in an unexpected twist of dramatic roles — by his own perseverance, a transcendent offensive game, and circumstances — became an antihero or, if not that, then the Oliver Twist of the NBA. Iverson started off as this hated or maybe misunderstood street urchin, his body a mass of taboo totems, tatted up the wazoo, daily braided, rapping foul and seeming to believe it, unlike rich "real" rappers with buttery wives with cascading hair-that-don't-hurt living in orchid-filled canyons in Hawaii. At least Iverson was authentic. People seemed to sense that, even if they didn't like him. And mostly they didn't. But put Iverson in a gritty locale like Philly, not in a piece of pussy like L.A., give him a Mutombo instead of a Shaq, have him overcome injuries and a televised pounding from giants twice his size, then send him up against an overwhelming force—Shaq, Kobe, and the Lakers . . . . We are Americans here. Love underdogs. We might like a story like that, get interested when Philly takes a game off the best team on the planet behind forty-eight from its pint-size star.

One school of thought says the twenty-six-year-old Iverson is as good as he's going to get. He can add only so much more muscle, if any, whereas Kobe has only begun to scratch the surface. Scary.

"Kobe's not physically mature yet," says his personal trainer, Joe Carbone, an ex-76ers employee. "When he finally matures, around age twenty-six, twenty-seven, it'll be like nothing you've ever seen before. We won't know what it'll be like until we see it. I know this. Whoever's relaxing right now, whoever's on vacation—they've already lost their chance." What people saw when they tuned in was pure dominance, the Lakers' methodical, relentless, cold-blooded execution of the Sixers, rather than inspired, athletic hoop. Kobe is capable of such play either way. What do you need? He can bring it. Scored forty-eight with sixteen boards against a good Sacramento team. Put down forty-five with ten rebounds against twin-towered San Antonio.

"Kobe has a first step like a point, handles like a point, has three-point shooting range, can guard ones and twos, can rebound with the long rifles, can block any shot. You might find a few good men who can do all that. But what separates Kobe, and Tracy McGrady too, is mental," says Orlando coach Doc Rivers. "It's their ability to understand the game and a toughness that's difficult to describe. They walk out there intending to dominate. It's hard to turn that off and on to protect people's feelings."

And yet . . . and yet . . . "Basketball is not the be-all and end-all," says Kobe while knocking back cheese and eggs scrambled light, white toast, bacon, and OJ with ice. He's on his way to lift with Joe Carbone. "Basketball is like life. But it is not life."

Let's be clear. Nobody in this world can take Kobe Bryant, nobody but Vanessa. Ol' Boy done been hit by a thunderbolt. Don't care how smart you are, kid, don't care if you are different from the rest of the ballers, mature beyond your years, deeper than people think, don't care if you look street but are more

European than street, don't matter if you've got no time for PlayStation, partying, or the other activities that distract your fellas in the NBA. In the end, you're still a man, and just a man and an athletic red-blooded American young man at that, so when you run across a Vanessa Laine, odds are you may get thunderbolted.

Vanessa is competitive. That's one reason Kobe dug her. She'd have to understand competition to be with him, to get him in the first place. She would have to be all that in order to stave off other honeys, not to mention reservations his father and mother and two sisters may have had. She would have to be good for Kobe to fall in love with her.

"Actually, we have it on tape, when we met for the very first time," Kobe says. He is smiling. "We were shooting this video for my hip-hop CD. Her mother was with her. A video director named Diane Martell had invited her to be in the video. So I was introducing myself to everybody. I tapped her on the shoulder and said, 'Hi. I'm Kobe.' She said 'Hi. I'm Vanessa.' I looked at her." Kobe tries to re-create the look—it is reminiscent of the look on the face of young Al Pacino when he first laid eyes on the peasant girl Appolonia in *The Godfather*. "After I met her," Kobe says, "I was like, 'Aight, I'm out.' There was something pure about her, something innocent. I couldn't forget her. Didn't try."

They were to be married in 2000, but, well, suffice it to say there are all kinds of triangles to negotiate in life, and they are all hard to learn how to execute. Kobe and Vanessa got it done in April of this year, playoff time, seeming to (inevitably!) alienate themselves from his family. One of his families. The Lakers were pleased. Maybe now Kobe would think of somebody besides Kobe. But people find it curious that Kobe's parents, Joe and Pam, were noticeably absent from the NBA Finals. Not in L.A., where they had lived for four years, nor in Philly, the city to which they've now returned.

"What is the price of fame?" Kobe asks. "It's being expected to play like the king of the world every single night against competition so good people don't even know. Being expected to act in a certain way. Know certain things before it would be possible for me to know them. But it's not like there's this overwhelming price to pay. It's the loss of privacy."

And what is there to gain for a man with a $71 mil contract and more than that in endorsements to reveal himself, to spin himself? It's not as though he needs the positioning. If you are Kobe Bryant, you are a complex man, not the kind who can be measured at a glance, so people misunderstand you, people you know and care about. There isn't anything you can say to make those close to you understand, let alone the rest. Your game was forged in solitude. You are young, so you are going to make mistakes. This is part of the making of a man. If it were me or you and a national hookup wanted to know where our daughter goes to elementary school, we might be less than expansive on the subject.

People like to talk about what they know. Kobe Bryant knows

basketball. He doesn't know what his private life is going to be like yet. He just got one.

In the end, the reason we care about all the gossip is that he takes our breath away; flies through the air at incredible angles and speeds, beats guys from the wing off the bounce, two dribbles max and right to the hole, has the made hops of life. Boy skies. F'real. *Whoo!* In an eye blink, with no flex span, hardly any knee bend, all lift. Hits PENTHOUSE and rises above the Tim Duncans, David Robinsons, and Dikembe Mutombos of the NBA, who are seven feet tall and doing their best leaping jobs themselves, stretching above the rack, twelve, thirteen feet up at their highest points. And still Kobe rises, flies over the top and through them, smoke through a keyhole, breathing fire from sharp flared nostrils, clearing our collective sinuses, racing pulses, then—boom! Throwdown. The Destroyer. The Finisher.

"Kobe Bryant is the primary offensive threat in the league," says Lakers owner Jerry Buss, who has overseen the installation of two dynasties, the Showtime Lakers of the '80s and the Great Lakers of this decade. In 1981, Buss signed Magic Johnson to a then historic $25 million deal that he paid off in ten years. That's chicken feed now. Bryant is working off a six-year deal with an out after the 2003-04 season, an out he'll never need. "I can't imagine a scenario where Kobe would ever get away," says Buss. He likes the ring of Laker for life.

—GQ, October 2001

GODS&
MONSTERS

BILLY
BASEBALL

The kind of hard-hitting and even harder-running game that manager Billy Martin brought to the Oakland A's in 1980 not only changed the fortunes of that franchise, but also the way the game itself was played. In this 1981 column from The Oakland Tribune, *Wiley gave Martin's ferocious new brand of baseball a name that still resonates today: Billy Ball.*

The air around the A's is much headier than that which shrouds the Giants. With the Giants, the catcher can't throw and conversation is endured painfully if at all. With the A's everything is chatter and pepper and kicking a little tail. I think it's Billy baseball.

Even the A's uniforms have a cheeriness about them, especially when compared to the Giants' Halloween mock-up. What was once Finley's white-shoed circus is now downright tasteful. Billy Martin wears his tiny golden cross beneath the bar of the Old English A that adorns the capital. He's very efficient about uniform dress and so are the players. Billy ball.

The A's are even much more fun on the field. Billy baseball is stealing and bunting at the same time, hoping the third baseman fields the bunt and the shortstop covers second: enabling the runner to possibly gain third base, or at least make threatening gestures.

Billy baseball is stealing home. Billy ball says a squeeze play a day keeps the shutouts away. The A's have tried the squeeze six times this spring. It has only worked three times, but it has never failed to be exciting for the people in the seats, which is the very best part of it.

One thing about Billy ball. It's low-profile. Martin says so in the papers. Who's going to cross him? Two of my best (only) sources looked at me like I was crazy when I asked who had been waived the other day. I'm sure they knew I would find out anyway, shortly, but they stayed mum, changing the subject expertly everytime I seized an opening.

Solidarity is great thing, but if writers are strictly limited to balls and strikes, well, television takes care of that news rather quickly. Talk about scooped. Newspapers offer depth and quotes and analysis/commentary. Martin calls it "like *Confidential* magazine." But locker-room stories are a part of baseball, too. It all depends on your viewpoint and employer.

"Managing can take a lot out of you," says Martin from Scottsdale Stadium quarters. "You can be happy one day and the next day you can't eat. They say a manager is five or ten games. I say he's worth more than that. He makes out the lineup everyday, doesn't he?

"There's a lot of guys who manage by the book. They say, 'If I do it by the book then nobody can second guess me.' Then they wonder why they get fired."

The A's are a kind of exhilaration not because of a man, but because of an attitude. Billy baseball.

"You can make a mistake," said a young infielder, "But you better not make the same mistake twice."

It is hard to say who has been helped the most by Billy Ball. But you can say that Matt Keough is one good looking pitcher (emphasis on the pitcher) this spring. And there are other starters who have looked just as good.

Keough, you will recall, pitched in abominably tough luck last year, finally gaining headlines because he lost fourteen straight games. But as the gnarled ones say, you wouldn't get the chance to lose that many if you weren't good.

Keough recalled a game last year in Seattle. He relishes his horror stories, it seems, and will probably one day revel his grandchildren with the epic of his tribulations before the dawn of Billy ball.

"You know how the Seattle ballpark is," said Keough. "The ball flies out of there. Well, it was a 0-0 game in the eighth inning. I was ahead of Leon Roberts 1-2. I threw him a breaking ball and he was looking for it and he knocked the hell out of it. I lost 1-0. The next day we hit five homers."

No wonder Keough admits he was tentative last year, unwilling to extend himself early or be aggressive if he happened to still be in there late. Billy baseball says defense makes pitching, of course. Some things are done by the book.

In a spring game against Seattle, Keough had a shutout going and Roberts came up. Keough got ahead of him, 1-2. Fastball? No. Struck him out on the breaking ball. 2-0, A's. You can't guess with Billy ball.

"The difference was this time I had burned his lips on the preceding pitch with a fastball," said Keough, smiling.

A man asked Keough what he would do if he started out this year with another losing streak.

"Mister, I can't lose," Keough said.

"Nothing worries me about this team. I refuse to be negative about any part of it. I won't run scared from anything. We can beat California. They've got the superstars, but we can beat them."

—Billy Martin

Billy baseball. If it were a fever, the A's would be an epidemic. There's another name for it. Confidence.

—The Oakland Tribune, March 23, 1980

ME AND
DOCTOR J.

Long before Lebron or Michael or even Magic owned the hardwood, there was Doctor J., Julius Erving. But as Wiley laments in this 1981 Oakland Tribune *column, the once high-flying Doctor, whom he considered "the Ali of basketball," had fallen to earth in recent years, though Madison Avenue would never let fans know it.*

A letter came today. It was about basketball and from Sausalito, of all places. The letter writer is named Denis DiPhillips, and he was very upset because I had written this past Tuesday that Julius Erving, Philadelphia's Doctor J., is overrated.

"How can you overrate the best player in the game?" is what Denis DiPhillips wanted to know.

The letter reminded me of my history with Julius Erving. How dare I, indeed.

I owe a lot to Doctor J. I owe basketball awareness to him. Doctor J opened my eyes to the game the way Elgin Baylor opened older eyes. The Doctor made me hold my breath. More importantly you might say the Doctor got me this job.

It was like this. When I first came to *The Oakland Tribune* six eventful years ago, those making decisions around here weren't about to just let me come in and have my say in print. There were certain initiation rites to go through. They lasted a long time, and they might have gone on and on without end were it not for the Doctor.

When the ABA merged with the NBA in 1976, not many staffers at *The Tribune* had ever seen or heard of Dr. Erving of the New York Nets. I was shocked and appalled. I was from an ABA town. I had seen what the Doctor could do to people, to hoops, to entire buildings. I knew he could bring them all down with one magnificent swoop. I asked those making decisions if I could write a story about him. They said, "Sure, kid," and were relieved that they didn't have to do it.

Well, I wrote that story. And another. And another. How dare I, indeed.

The NBA was the nest of my first beat. The Warriors were the first team I had all to myself. Unfortunately, they weren't very good. Fortunately, I got to see and talk to Doctor J.

The first time was difficult. The 76ers came here. Julius had his usual great game and was his usual personable self afterward only there is no locker-room time in which to casually converse with Erving. He is the quintessential media star. Everybody wants and he gives. So my first interview with the Doctor was a piece-meal arrangement by necessity. I shouted to be heard and he shouted to answer. I worked my way to the front because I wanted him to remember my face.

He did. He forgot the name. I wanted to tell him I was bad with names too the next time I saw him which was in Philadelphia later in the year.

I asked him to come to the Spectrum early for an interview,

then was late myself. He had come early which was not a small thing for him to do.

"Where were you?" he asked.

"Got lost." I lied.

His eyebrows knit, and I thought that I had lost my chance, but I stayed with him through the gruffness, and pretty soon he was smiling and making wry and astute comments. He was the Doctor again, the one whose courtside manner was as great as his artful drives to the ring.

I have never seen the Doctor be anything but personable, even though every forward in the league psyches himself into top shape when Julius comes to town. For him, every game is a playoff game. He's the gunslinger they all want to kill.

The current knock on the Doctor is that he hasn't won it all, as if he could do it alone.

The Doctor tried. He went to the finals twice. George McGinnis, Bill Walton, and one missed jumper kept him from the title in 1977. The Lakers, the best team ever, kept him from it last year.

Now, the NBA hypes the Doctor shamelessly. There are others who deserve publicity, too. But the NBA is fixed on the Doctor. The NBA knows it can count on him. It knows he won't go turn Sphinx or not show up for games, or pout.

I once said that five Julius Ervings could defeat five of any other player who ever lived. Now I'm not so sure, but five Doctors against five Magics or five Marqueses would be a hell of a go.

For me, he is still the most exciting player who ever lived. He made the slam-dunk a weapon and an art form. And he may yet win it all.

I have seen the Doctor perform the most amazing athletic feats possible—like his one-in-a-million-flying-hanging scoop shot in the 1980 finals against the Lakers—and I have also seen him answer every numbing demand the media, the fans, and the league itself placed on him.

I said he was overrated because the NBA Madison Avenue types should spread the hype around to other deserving stars. I said he was overrated because his outside shot is erratic. But he is overrated only in relative terms, only because he is rated so very high above the others.

He is not that high above them, not anymore. But he is the one who brought them up to his level, the one who said reaching the stars was possible. At thirty-two, he is the still the Ali of basketball.

One player is always overrated in basketball. It takes five to play well. Julius will tell you that himself. All you have to do is ask him. I did.

—The Oakland Tribune, February 28, 1981

A MONUMENTAL
STREAK

When Cal Ripken played in his 1,308th consecutive game in 1990 to move into second place on the all-time list, Wiley commemorated the feat with this profile in Sports Illustrated. *With Lou Gehrig's streak still more than 800 games away and seemingly far out of reach, Wiley noted that "Ripken would need five more seasons to do the breaking, and nobody really expects that to happen. But the world will be watching."*

O n the afternoon of April 19, Calvin E. Ripken Jr. glided onstage to play shortstop for the Baltimore Orioles in their 1990 home opener against the Detroit Tigers. Cheers of affection cascaded down from the fans at Memorial Stadium.

Memorial Stadium is a relic, to be consigned to the past in the spring of 1992 when the Orioles move into their new waterfront home near Camden Yards. People say that as a boy Babe Ruth played in the neighborhood where the new ballpark will be built, and one day people will say that Ripken played there, too. But these remembrances of Ripken are likely to be unspectacular, | un-Ruthian; they will be hazy, imprecise—shadows of a big man playing shortstop with a stately but eager cool.

In that home opener at Memorial Stadium, Ripken was, as usual, most noticeable for the things he did not do. He did not make an error. He did not mess up a double play. After the game, Ripken played no clubhouse pranks and kicked no watercoolers. He didn't rip the manager or offer clever quips to reporters or trade noisy jokes with his teammates. He dressed quietly and drove his new Lincoln Continental to his recently acquired spread near suburban Reisterstown, Maryland, to his wife, Kelly—they've been married only two-and-a-half years—and his daughter, Rachel, born just last November. Wife, daughter, house, car: Their combined longevity in Ripken's life is less than that of The Streak.

Barring rainout or other disruption, Ripken, on Tuesday of this week, will have played in his 1,308th consecutive major league game, surpassing Yankee and Red Sox shortstop Everett Scott's streak, set from 1916 to 1925. Ripken has played in every Baltimore game since May 30, 1982. In a stretch from June 5, 1982, to Sept. 14, 1987, he played 8,243 consecutive innings. Over the course of The Streak, he has played, through Sunday, in 12,897 of his team's 12,939 innings, or 99.68 percent of them. In the eight years of The Streak, he has married, had a child, seen his life evolve and change. In those eight years, the Orioles' lineup card has seen a complete transformation, except for one constant: SS—Cal Ripken Jr.

Yet, by passing Scott, Ripken moves only into second place on the all-time list. There is, of course, still the matter of Lou Gehrig and his 2,130 consecutive games played, the record they say will never be broken. Ripken would need five more seasons to do the breaking, and nobody really expects that to happen. But the world will be watching. For all his mastery as an athlete, Ripken is being measured by time, and he is a man who feels imprisoned by it. "The game never ends," says the twenty-nine-year-old Ripken, running his hands through hair now shot with gray, "because there's always another one."

For Ripken, ball games come not in sets of three or four or seven, but in sets of 162. In the age of the space shuttle, the tanning salon and the twenty-second sound bite, how can this be? More important, how long can it continue? "There's no pressure on Cal," says his father, Cal Ripken Sr., Baltimore's third base coach, a man who seems to be constructed of rawhide lines pulled taut. "No pressure in it. You go to the ballpark and do the best job you possibly can that day. Cal always wanted to be as good a professional baseball player as possible."

And what of The Streak? When will it end? "I have no idea," says Cal Sr.

On the final weekend of last season's American League East race, during a Friday game between the eventual division champions, the Toronto Blue Jays, and the Orioles, destined for second, the broadcast booth in Toronto's SkyDome was filled with commentary.

"The problem I have with Cal is that he changes his stance so much," said the Oriole living legend, Brooks Robinson. "He's trying to pull everything."

"The man of many stances," said Jim Palmer, the ace of Oriole aces. "The question about Cal is, after playing all those games, is he getting tired?"

At the time, Ripken, a big man who is still called Junior, was playing in game No. 1,248 and, consequently or not, having a weak at bat. He flied out to center.

In a season in which he batted only .257, it somehow was over-looked that Ripken slugged 21 homers to become the first short-stop in history to have eight straight 20-home run seasons, supplanting Mr. Cub, Ernie Banks, in the record books. He would complete the year with a 47-game errorless streak and only eight errors all told. (The major league record for fewest errors in a season by a shortstop—six—was set last year by Toronto's Tony Fernandez.) Ripken fielded at a .990 percentage and led major league shortstops in putouts, assists, double plays, and total chances. He led all shortstops in homers and RBIs—93—for the sixth time in seven years. In July '89, he started his sixth consec-utive All-Star Game, another league record.

Ripken is six-foot-four and weighs 220 pounds—"So I should be able to drive the ball out of the ballpark occasionally," he says, as if any big man is naturally obliged to do such things. Not so easi-ly explained is his skill afield. Ripken is one of the biggest men ever to play shortstop, let alone play the position so consistently and gracefully. As of Sunday, he had committed but one error this season and had a 54-game errorless streak.

One might expect that in Baltimore this velvet-gloved iron man, this long-ball shortstop, would enjoy the stature of local hero. That is not the case. Ripken is rigorously roasted on radio call-in talk shows all around Chesapeake Bay, chided for the RBIs he didn't get, accused of not being a leader, bad-mouthed for his sub-.220 batting average this season, even second-guessed over his determination to play every day. The implications are obvious: Junior is pressing. Maybe Junior could use a rest. You're tired, aren't you, Junior?

"Not particularly," says Ripken. "But I hear them."

The skeptical voices are raised elsewhere, too. In late May, Patrick Reusse, a columnist for the Minneapolis *Star Tribune*, put Ripken on his "All-Washed-Up" team (prompting a quick and angry TV response from Palmer). In a more reasoned critique, Steve Hirdt of the Elias Sports Bureau recently said, "Ripken's pursuit [of The Streak] is counterproductive both to himself and his team." A former Baltimore teammate, veteran catcher Rick Dempsey, suggested from Los Angeles last year that taking an occasional day off might do Junior good. "Well, I'll never know," says Ripken, jaw locked. "It'll never happen."

Ripken's batting average so far this season—it bottomed out at .208 on June 5—hasn't done much to quiet his detractors. But he still is among the team leaders in homers (seven), runs (33) and RBIs (30). He quickly dismisses those who point to his batting average. "Two-out singles to right with nobody on," Ripken says, his lip curling ever so slightly. "Do they drive in runs? I'm here to drive the ball. I won't cut down on my swing to hit .280 so the critics can be happy and the Orioles can finish fifth."

Ripken has never been anything but an Oriole. In July of 1988, during a 107-loss season for the O's and not long after Cal Sr. was replaced as the Baltimore manager, Ripken passed up free agency and re-signed with the Orioles for three years at around $2.45 million per. Ripken is an Oriole for life, and to some Baltimore minds that makes him community property. Junior, they say, if you aren't hitting, you must be tired. Maybe it's time to sit down before you let us down.

There are other voices, though. "I'm the batting instructor and I'm not complaining," says Tom McCraw, Baltimore's hitting coach. "Cal is a superb athlete and a great pro. He'll hit. What you can't see is how Cal dominates the mental side of the game. You'd have to watch him every day, and watch him close."

On the evening of Sept. 6, 1989, the Cleveland Indians were in the process of drubbing Baltimore 9-0. The blowout gave Oriole manager Frank Robinson a chance to see what his bonus-baby rookie pitcher, Ben McDonald, could do. With the Indians ahead 4-0 in the top of the third inning, McDonald made his major league debut. The situation he faced was runners at first and third, one out, and Cory Snyder at the plate. Ripken jogged to the mound to greet the kid.

"Make sure you come to a stop, Ben," Ripken told him. "Let us get the outs for you. That's what we're here for."

McDonald's first pitch was just outside to the righthanded Snyder, who hit a slow two-hopper back up the middle. Ripken, having seen catcher Bob Melvin's sign, had positioned himself slightly shallower and more to his left than usual. His big hands seemed to wave at each other as he caught the ball and flipped toward second to begin a 6-4-3 double play. McDonald had recorded two outs with his first major league pitch.

"I had a couple of balks in the minors," said McDonald later. "He [Ripken] knew that. And he wanted me to know that if the ball was hit back to me, he'd be covering. I'd heard he knows the game. Even minor leaguers know that about Junior."

"The first and last rule of baseball, as I was taught it," says Ripken, "is to catch the ball, then to know what to do with it once you do. You have to know the hitters, how they hit with two strikes, how they hit with two balls, how they adjust to what the pitcher is trying to do to them. Not from scouting reports, necessarily. I've formed that bank myself, by noticing what's been going on around me all my life.

"It comes down to you gotta play games. You gotta play as many games as you can. Since there are so many possible plays, you can't get it all unless you're there every day. You can't get it from a book. You play games. And after you play so many games, experience so many different ground balls, runners, hitters, and situations, you learn to prepare for each hitter, each count, each pitch, each option—even each potential injury."

Baseball can be a dangerous game of hard swings, slung bats, high spikes, purpose pitches, brawls, inrushing outfielders, and outrushing infielders. Ripken's streak is made more amazing by the fact that he plays shortstop, which means he must make the pivot at second. "It doesn't matter who's down there," says Los

Angeles Dodger slugger Kirk Gibson. "Whoever turns the pivot has got to pay."

"My size helps me on the pivot," says Ripken. "And technique, too. When I'm coming across the bag, I use the 'flip.' The flip [a sidearm toss] is my throw, for accuracy and consistency reasons. More accurate. Less wear and tear. Rick Burleson used to throw everything hard, and he tore his rotator cuff. My throw and my size protect me on the pivot. The runners are in front of me. They will pull back, one way or another. But there have been a couple of, uh, incidents of collision."

Darrell Miller, a former catcher in the Baltimore organization, remembers a game a few years ago when he was playing with the California Angels. Miller barreled into second base as Ripken was making the pivot. Sometimes Ripken can throw, leap, and tuck all in one motion. This time he took the throw, fired, and braced. Miller, expecting to intersect with an airborne Ripken, instead ran into a tree of a man and had his wind knocked out. Ripken barely bounced off the bag. A moment later, the 210-pound Miller gasped and said, "Hey, you all right?" Junior smiled. So did Miller before saying, "I can't believe it was me asking you."

Only once has The Streak been seriously threatened by an injury. On the second day of the 1985 season, against the Texas Rangers, Ripken began to move toward second base for a pickoff play against the Ranger runner, Gary Ward. "My spikes got caught on top of the bag," says Ripken. "I heard a pop, felt the bang. I said, 'That's it, it's broken.' [Baltimore trainer] Richie

Bancells taped my [left] ankle up tight, and I led off the next inning. The next day, it swelled like a balloon."

But the Orioles had an exhibition against the Naval Academy that day. The ankle was not broken, and the swelling subsided, so Ripken, who says his ankles are his weakest physical feature, did not miss a game. The Streak lived on.

Ozzie Guillen of the Chicago White Sox is considered a better glove man with better range than Ripken. Fernandez of the Blue Jays has an arm the equal of Ripken's and better range. Ozzie Smith of the St. Louis Cardinals surely gets to balls Ripken could never reach. But Ripken has led American League shortstops in assists for five of the last seven seasons. He must be getting to something.

"Yeah, he's getting to me," says Yankee owner George Steinbrenner. "He's hurt me enough. He's one of the most consummate athletes I've seen in all of sports."

Ripken gets not only to most struck balls but also to trains, planes, cars, buses, charity fund-raisers, Baltimore adult literacy campaign functions, taping sessions for fast-food-chain commercials, Drink Milk photo shoots, trade shows, media interviews, ball games, and, eventually, back to the struck ball itself—all while avoiding the random household or infield accident as well as debilitating illnesses. "Certain pitchers give some guys the flu, you know," says Frank Robinson. "Not Cal. In my day, we played because we didn't know any better; we thought the guy on the bench would take our jobs. Cal plays with that hunger. Today, it's a whole new game, a new breed. Usually, today's game is almost a platoon system. But Cal's name"—Robinson smiles—"is stenciled on all my lineup cards."

Most everybody else in this working world calls in sick every now and then. "It's been said I'm a prisoner of The Streak," says Ripken, as if to mean he doesn't disagree with this assessment yet will not offer it up for any public sympathy. Are you a prisoner of The Streak, Cal? "I don't feel all that free, if that's what you mean," he says.

Ripken naturally shies from public scrutiny, and displays few of the tics or foibles that might invite attention—unless pounding the brewskies from time to time, or not gladly suffering fools or criticism, or falling into an occasional lurch of profanity constitute terrible character flaws. But spare him any adulation.

"Superstar? Oh, no. I don't know if I want that," he says. "I've seen what that can do. Anyway, I don't think I stack up with the great talents in the league. I have talent, no doubt. My advantage is that I know the game well. The reason is that I grew up in it and had a good teacher in my father. I'm sure that whatever I am as a man and as a ballplayer comes from the way I was raised."

The foul tip smashed into Cal Sr.'s upper arm, and the pain nearly made him break his crouch. A career minor leaguer, Cal Sr. looked up at the sky over Daytona Beach, Florida, on this summer day in 1961 and grimaced. He didn't know the technical term for what had happened until the doctors told him: It was a bruised deltoid muscle, which had been knocked out of alignment with the bone.

Nine years earlier, in 1952, he had decided to become a pro base-ball player even though he was only about five-foot-eleven and 170 pounds. Cal Sr. was a catcher who was born with a good right arm. All the foul tips off his fingers and hands, all the charging base runners, all the curves he had just missed hitting on the sweet part of the bat didn't matter as long as he could throw.

After that foul tip, he couldn't. "So that was it for me as a play-er right then," says Cal Sr., from the modest, five-bedroom wood-frame home in Aberdeen, Maryland, where the Ripken children, Ellen, Cal Jr., Fred, and Billy, grew up. "Cal was born in 1960," says Cal Sr. "I was in Fox Cities at the time—Class B. After I got hurt in '61, I started right into managing. Leesburg, Appleton, Elmira, Rochester, Dallas, Bal'mer. All with the Bal'mer organization. The Bal'mer organization is a good organization."

Cal Sr. was not about to push baseball on Cal Jr. "That decision was made by him," says the elder Ripken. "Too many people in the world don't enjoy what they do for a living. If you don't enjoy your living, you've lost the battle right there."

"Baseball took my dad away from me," says Cal Jr. "He left at one o'clock every day on the days he was at home, and he was gone completely half the time, on the road. I learned very early that if I wanted to see my dad at all, I would have to go to the ball-park with him. He'd put me in a uniform and send me to the out-field and say, 'Don't come into the infield, son. It's too dangerous in there. You can get hurt bad. Shag flies or whatever. And always keep your eyes open.' I still wouldn't get to see him that much, but I'd ask questions on our drives to and from the ballpark. I liked those drives."

When Cal Sr. was on the road, Cal Jr. and his younger brother Billy got baseball nourishment from their mother. When Billy played for Aberdeen High, he pitched a game in 30 degrees weather and wind so strong he was blown off the mound. The only spectator was a woman with a baseball cap pulled down over her ears, Vi Ripken.

"She's a strong lady," says Billy. "She had to be. While my dad was gone, she was there. Later on, after I decided to be a professional ballplayer, I'd call home and ask Dad for advice. Mom would get on first and tell me what I was doing wrong. I'd tell her to put Dad on the phone. Dad would get on and repeat what she said."

There seemed to be no end to the boys' appetite for baseball. "I always had a hunger to learn the game," says Cal Jr. "I had the hunger to play that all kids have, but it was more than that. When my dad went to coach in Baltimore, I was going into high school. I had the chance to sit and talk with Bumbry, Belanger, Singleton, Grich, Baylor, DeCinces. My favorite time was after the game. I was like a reporter. I'd review game charts and have all my questions ready. Why did this guy steal? Why didn't the catcher throw on this play? I would fire the questions at my dad. He'd tell me why everything happened. I'd question the player the next day. Why did you do that? What were you thinking?

"My bedtime stories were about foul tips splintering up fingers, and taping them together, spitting a little tobacco juice on them and saying to the umpire, 'Let's play.' Hearing those stories, it was like my dad would have had to break his back to stay out of the lineup."

Cal Jr. now tells his own stories about his father's toughness. When he was sixteen and Billy was twelve, a heavy snowfall blocked the roads around the house in Aberdeen. Cal Sr. rigged up a plow to an old tractor, but the battery was dead. "Dad starts to hand-crank it," says Junior, "and the engine backfires. The crank flies up and opens up a gash on his forehead and I'm saying let's go to the hospital. My dad says, 'Just go on home.' He's got an oily rag held up to his head. He goes into the bathroom, slaps a couple of butterfly bandages on it, goes back out and starts the tractor and plows the snow off the road. That's my dad. That should help make you understand a little."

A little about the son and the father? About playing with pain, about playing up to a father's expectations? "The fact that my dad is in the clubhouse with me has helped me," says Junior. "But I don't know if I'm expected to do the same as he did. I feel a certain amount of pressure about that, no question."

Baltimore made Cal Jr. a second-round draft pick in 1978, and he signed quickly. He came up to the Orioles in 1981, in 1982 he was the American League rookie of the year, and the next year the O's won the World Series. For a while the game seemed so easy. "In the beginning, it was," he says. "Playing behind Palmer, Mike Flanagan, Scott McGregor, Dennis Martinez. You play behind them once, they were such excellent pitchers, you already had a feel for what they were trying to do. Back then, I was just a cog on the team, helping the offense run. We had Bumbry, Roenicke, Lowenstein, Singleton. We had Eddie in the middle of the lineup."

"That's just the way it was back then in the Baltimore organization," says Eddie Murray, now the first baseman for the Dodgers. "Cal came in after I'd been up five years. He came to me and asked things, and I'd try to help him. Things we all go through. The period came for Cal where he was taking the first pitch a lot, slumping a little. I told him always to be ready to spin on the first-pitch fastball. I liked Cal because he was a gamer, always was a gamer. But back then the Baltimore organization was different."

For a time Cal Jr. could see it all in his mind: His brother Billy coming up to play second base for the O's, their father becoming the manager, and Cal and Eddie crushing extra-base hits and leading Baltimore to another World Series triumph. But the Baltimore organization fell upon hard times. Its seventeen-year streak of winning records ended in 1985. The next three years were nightmarish.

Billy did come up, in 1987, the same year Cal Sr. became manager. Some observers said it was a package deal, that Cal Jr. would have declared himself a free agent as soon as he could if his father hadn't gotten the job. After finishing sixth in the

American League East in 1987 with a 67-95 record, Baltimore began 1988 with a 0-21 mark. Cal Sr. was replaced six games into the season. Following his father's dismissal, Junior was expected to show up and play ball as if nothing had happened, and that was what he did.

"Anybody who says Cal had anything to do with me getting hired is a liar," says Cal Sr. "After I was fired, there was nothing for him to say about that either. His job is to go to the ballpark and play. He doesn't have time to get caught up in anything else."

"Cal got through it," says Murray. "He'll be fine. He doesn't have anything to worry about—except having somebody on base and having somebody behind him who can hit. We had some good years together, some great years. But things went bad, and I got blamed."

After having been the most productive run producer in the major leagues in the '80s, Murray left Baltimore in a cloud of acrimony, traded in the winter of 1988. "I know Jackie Robinson went through hell," says Murray, "because I know what I heard around Baltimore from so-called fans. I can't tell you what it did to me. I've never shot a gun in my life, but I was told things that made me want to go get a gun and kill somebody. I couldn't talk to anyone but Cal."

"Eddie's been hurt," says Cal Jr. "We live in a world where success is determined by statistics. Eddie and I would have good stats going in every September. But at one point, players from other teams came out and told us that their pitchers were fined if they gave Eddie or me a pitch to hit and we beat them. It's hard to be productive like that. In all good baseball sense, you should take your walks. But it's hard to deal with, because you want to hit. So you start to expand your strike zone, and at the major league level you can't do that unless your name is Kirby Puckett. Eddie Murray set a higher standard for me while he was here. I benefited from playing with him, and hitting in front of him. I didn't fully realize how much until he left. But I know he's been hurt."

One gets the feeling that everything Cal Jr. says about Murray is steeped in the knowledge that something similar could happen to him. Perhaps that's why people say Ripken has no personality. He gives them none to feed off.

It is the spring of 1990, and the Orioles are taking infield practice at Miami Stadium. Third base coach Cal Sr. hits ground balls to the infielders. He hits them harder to Cal Jr. than to anyone else. Junior smiles while he picks them up easily, as if they were dandelions. The O's enter the dugout for an exhibition game with the New York Mets. Some Baltimore fans are near one corner of the dugout.

"Hey, get Billy's autograph!"

"Nah, don't get his autograph. He sucks! Tell him to sign Darryl Strawberry's name on it!"

"Cal! How 'bout a picture?"

"Jeez, I ask Cal for a picture, he turns the other way!"

Cal and Billy trot out to their positions and stand next to each other during the national anthem. Cal wears number 8, Billy number 3.

"You can tell by their asses they ain't the same!" says a fan.

In the first inning, with runners on first and second and one out, Mike Marshall hits a spinner to Billy, who makes sure of the play and tosses slowly to Cal to get the out at second; Cal fires to first but just misses getting the runner. "You kind of threw me a changeup," Cal tells Billy.

"I know. Wanted the sure out," replies Billy. Cal nods.

"Oh sure," says Billy later, "I hear 'em saying I'll never be as good as my brother. Sometimes I want to yell back at them, 'No s—.' They think I don't know that? They're telling the truth, so how can I get mad? Sure, I'd like to get in eight years or so. But I know my brother would never say, 'I want my brother here to play with me.' He wouldn't do that.

"We're two different people. On the field we're not brothers. We're teammates. My brother is a superstar. I just wanted to be a good professional baseball player. It wasn't a decision I made. That's all I ever remember wanting." Cal listens to his brother, saying nothing.

"Gehrig's streak is a record that has grown greater and greater as it has grown older," says Robert Creamer, baseball historian and author.

On May 2, 1939, at Briggs Stadium in Detroit, Gehrig's streak ended. The Iron Horse trudged out to home plate, even in his debilitated condition—he would be dead two years later, a victim of ALS, or "Lou Gehrig's disease"—to deliver the lineup card to the umpires. Batting eighth for the Yankees would be first baseman Babe Dahlgren.

The moment was captured by an eyewitness named Art Hill, in his 1980 book *I Don't Care If I Never Come Back*: "The disease . . . had already begun to cripple him, because I clearly remember that he walked slowly and rather stiffly toward the waiting group of umpires. I also remember that the fans stood and applauded for what seemed like a long time but was probably about two minutes . . . . The standing ovation has become meaningless in an era when people do not know the difference between a good thing and a great thing."

Gehrig's streak was a great thing, to be sure. One could argue, though, that in certain ways Gehrig had an easier time of it than Ripken does now. Gehrig played first base, had no night games or West Coast road trips, and sat out late innings in many Yankee blowouts. Ripken will hear none of that talk. "Lou Gehrig was a great ballplayer," he says. "I can't do what he did. I can only do what I can."

Cal Jr. has hit better than .300 twice, in 1983 and 1984, but his average has been in a decline over the last four years, falling to a career-low 252 in 1987. He has struggled mightily at the plate this season, with no one resembling Murray batting behind him. And the critics have intensified their watch.

"People don't understand," says Cal Jr. "And what can I tell them? Have you heard the radio call-in shows?"

His comfort is now found at home, with Kelly and Rachel. "It's a learning process all over again," he says of life with his infant daughter. "It's totally different. It changes you. And you know, you find out that as hard as you've worked for one thing, the only thing that really matters is life itself. If I have a bad day, and people heckle me, and the radio shows rip me, I go home to my little girl. She thinks I'm perfect.

"I stayed in Baltimore because everything was in place and secure. But I learned from Eddie. Things are fine, but I know things change."

—Sports Illustrated, June 18, 1990

WILL HISTORY
REPEAT ITSELF FOR MJ?

Michael Jordan didn't exactly ask for any career advice, but that didn't stop Wiley from offering some in this 2003 ESPN.com column. Presenting Jordan with the cautionary tale of Babe Ruth's post-playing days, Wiley makes the case that MJ should be as fierce in his front-office ambition as he was on the court.

M

ichael Jordan is often called the Babe Ruth of basketball.

Once that was a compliment. Now, it's a warning sign. Big-time.

Michael Jordan has to sit on his ego and make a shrewd play, not tomorrow, but right now. He can't make a power play, because he's no longer in a position of power. One has-been athlete is like any other. He can't intimidate, point a finger at teammates, frown and shoot a game-winning fade. No announcer will say, "He did it again! He did it again! He did it again!" about Jordan's next front-office experience—if he has a next front-office experience—and if some announcer does say it, it'll mean more trouble in Mudville.

Babe Ruth was once the Home Run King Who Saved Baseball. And yet, when his playing days were done, nobody wanted any part of him—as a manager, executive, or anything else. There was closet resentment among those who were not in his sphere of influence with the Yankees, and resentment about the way he had dominated baseball. His brusque manner hadn't worn well on opposing teams and Yankee management.

After being released by the Yankees, the team whose image he had created, in the sense of their homer-hitting, world championship-winning swagger (much as Jordan had created the Chicago Bulls), Ruth came in with the Boston Braves, his own version of the Washington Wizards, on what looked like (to a simple ballplayer) a sweetheart deal, much as Jordan looked to have one with the Wiz. Jordan was off somewhere minding his own considerable ego when AOL magnate Ted Leonsis bought a piece of the Wiz off Abe Pollin, who apparently isn't as senile as he looks.

Leonsis owns the majority of the Washington Capitals, a hockey team in a town that ices over for five days each year. He overpaid for a talented but non-competitive chump named Jaromir Jagr, just to bask in Jagr's past Stanley Cup glory. He also offered to bring Jordan into the fold of the Wizards, to run it, and for a piece of his piece of the action. Pollin acquiesced quietly. Jordan jumped at it, as he should have. But then, incredibly, he gave up his piece—he didn't appreciate its value, or thought he could get it back just for the asking—just to come back and play (!?), after some of his management moves were not immediately productive.

Quickly reverting to jock type, he snatched off his business suit to reveal his Superman cape, tattered by wear-and-tear though it was.

Abe Pollin just sat back. He saw his building, the MCI Center, sell out for two seasons, just as Leonsis's net worth dwindled like Ted

Turner's, as AOL took a swirly in the toilet of the stock market. Abe had the hole card. He still had 51 percent of the Wizards.

In 1935, Judge Emil Fuchs owned the majority share of the Boston Braves and had been struggling along with them for the better part of two decades, just as Abe Pollin did before Jordan came in. The Braves were mired in the American League second division in the 1920s and '30s, as the cocky Ruth's Yankees were winning fistfuls of world titles and Ruth set home run and marketing records and became a national icon.

The Bullets/Wizards were mired in the NBA Eastern Conference second division in the '80s and '90s, as the cocky Jordan's Bulls were winning fistfuls of world titles and Jordan won scoring titles and set marketing records and became a national icon.

Fuchs, like Pollin, had been losing cash. Somebody told Fuchs it would be a coup to get Ruth on board in 1935, once he had had "retired" from the Yankees. Fuchs said, of course he'd want Ruth to have an "official position" with the club (uh-huh) and added this: "He can play as often as he wants." Author Robert W. Creamer put it this way, in his superb book on Ruth: "Words like executive position, manager, next year, stock options, profits, ownership of the club caressed Ruth's ear . . . ." The Braves offered Ruth a salary, executive position as an officer of the corporation, assistant manager title, a share of the profits during the term of the contract, and an option to purchase some of the stock of the club.

Ruth jumped at it. Way too fast.

He jumped as a player jumps. He never saw the fine print coming.

Ruth joined the Braves. They drew big crowds. For a while. He had his last hurrah. For a while. Then the Braves settled back into the second division, and Ruth found that he and Fuchs did not get along at all. Once, he yelled at Fuchs, "You attend to your end of the business and I'll attend to mine! Mine is on the field!" Fuchs, knowing all along what he was going to do, persuaded Ruth to stay on as an active player through the western road trip in 1935. Teams had Babe Ruth Days planned. "You can't quit now," Fuchs said.

A few weeks later, Ruth, the greatest, most definitive baseball player who ever lived up until then, and even today one of the two or three best, was limping along hitting .155. He had one last day of glory in Pittsburgh, going 4-for-4 with three homers, six RBI. The Braves lost anyway, 11-7. (Jordan, for his part, became the first forty-year-old player to score 40 points in an NBA game; that, and two dollars, gets you on the subway, but not into any owner's box.)

The Braves traveling secretary and Ruth's wife Claire told him he should quit on the spot. "Can't do it," he said. "I promised that son of a bitch [Fuchs] I'd play in all the towns on this [May] trip."

The Braves were 10-27 when Ruth quit as a player. Immediately, Fuchs sent out a message: Ruth had been released as player and as assistant manager, and had been fired as vice-president. "I have given Ruth his unconditional release," Fuchs said in a written statement. "He's through with the Braves in every way."

So now it's just déjà vu all Pollin again.

I'm sure Jordan is unaware of this history; those who are unaware of history . . . oh hell, this isn't the History Channel, it's an R-Dub Page 2 column. These similarities are fascinating, but Jordan can step out of this "Twilight Zone" episode and stop making like Babe Ruth, and I can stop making like Rod Serling. What Jordan should do now is not pout, which, like Ruth, he is very good at, but act on his own behalf, and not wait for David Falk to tell him what's best, because Falk never saw this coming and he should have. Should've never let his best client give up his piece of a club. Never, as in: not ever. Now Jordan must act decisively, and act like a businessman, not some spoiled, petulant superstar athlete/artist (that "statement" he released, probably through David Falk, accomplished nothing).

"They treated him like a player," said Kenny the Sage on TNT.

Revenge is a dish best served during the NBA Finals. What Jordan should do is find out where Paul Silas will be staying in Sacramento and call him up. Silas is the best coach not currently employed in the NBA. Don Nelson, the Dallas head coach, in a shrewd preemptive strike, has brought Silas in as an "observer" or as a "consultant" with the Mavs. This came after Paul Silas was inexplicably fired by inexplicable Hornets owner George Shinn. Paul Silas is known to work wonders with teams, particularly with big men, having made the Hornets a threat team, and having turned center Jamal Magliore into one of hidden gems in the NBA. He has the respect of Baron Davis, which is more than, say,

Jeff Van Gundy or Tim Floyd can claim at this point. By bringing in Silas, Nelson, by happy coincidence, obviously doesn't have to worry about coaching against him, although it is true Nellie and Silas were once teammates on the Celtics, and Silas won't mind the checks continuing to come in, although decidedly smaller.

Jordan can make a better offer than that. He can say, "Look Paul, I know I screwed up my spot big-time in Washington, but I can get in with Charlotte as team president and director of basketball ops. I also can and will buy a piece. Bob Johnson won't give me a piece, like Ted Leonsis did. It was sort of found money for Ted anyway, with that stupid AOL windfall from Time-Warner. Yes, I should've recognized and appreciated the value of that piece. Live and learn. Bob Johnson has the first nickel he ever made. I'll have to buy my way back in. Cool. I know now what David Falk should've told me. Too much pride. So I turned down a big settlement from Abe, which I could've used to buy a piece of Charlotte. Good for Abe. I'll visit him soon. But I also know Eddie Tapscott well, and he's running the new shop down in Charlotte right now, but Eddie is a devotee of Red Holzman, who believed that, win or lose, you go home, have a tumbler of scotch, and forget it. Eddie will be flexible with us. We'll make him an offer he can't refuse. I think . . . know . . . Bob Johnson and I can cut a deal. I will do it only if you're part of my package as our coach, with a nice fat five-year contract and my backing and blessing. What do you say?" Silas has got to hear that.

Will Jordan do this? I don't know. Probably not. Michael Jordan doesn't do anything anybody else suggests. That always worked for him on the court. That's what's been killing him off of it.

I hope Michel Jordan won't continue to be the Babe Ruth of basketball. As Ruth could've told him, it ends kind of ugly.

—ESPN.com, May 8, 2003

WHITE LIES

A documentary about O.J. Simpson inspired Wiley to write a passionate column about the man he knew as both a player and a colleauge. (In 1989, the two men worked together on NBC's NFL Live.) Double-murder charges notwithstanding, to Wiley, Simpson's great crime was abandoning his role as a black role model when he was in his prime and then hiding behind the race card when he was on trial.

HBO's latest sports documentary *says* it's an examination of race relations throughout O.J. Simpson's life, a "Study in Black and White." Actually, it's a study in white. It toes a media party line that white is right and black is base. There are knowing lines within the documentary, but they are blunted by an overall naivete.

The documentary's most honest trait is its brevity—some 49 minutes in length. Why? Because, when you get down to it, at the center of O.J. Simpson, there was nothing there. Nada. If ever there was not only a colorless but soulless man, it was him.

Yet the documentary starts off with him saying, "I'm a black guy, always been a black guy, never been nothing but a black guy."

This is disingenuous. O.J. tried and almost succeeded at being everything but a black guy—and, more important, his own guy.

He fooled himself. He fooled white people. But he didn't fool very many black people. Not the ones who knew him well, anyway.

O.J. Simpson could be and often was base. Jim Brown knew it.

Harry Edwards knew it. His first wife Marguerite (whom he stole from his black "best friend," Al Cowlings) knew it. I learned it. To people like us, there was no arguing it.

But not to white people, especially the captains of industry Juice performed for. His off-screen antics made Stepin Fetchit look like Frederick Douglass.

No, we were all the difficult ones. We were the ones who didn't understand how to be, how to go along to get along. If a black man is grinning all the time, being obsequious, that is seen as some kind of righteousness; meanwhile, those seeing it that way never seem to understand that no person can live a life of mental duplicity for very long without something beginning to slip upstairs.

In the doc, former sociology professor at Cal-Berkeley Harry Edwards says Simpson, "bought the hype," because it brought him a rich lifestyle. Juice played long before the big multi-million dollar contracts. Yet he lived like a prince. Traits like self-respect, personal responsibility, personal excellence, not just on a playing field, and community responsibility and plain common sense have nothing to do with fooling people.

O.J. fooled a lot of people.

Few of them were black.

One of my writing colleagues—and I mean no disrespect—got juked by O.J. worse than any UCLA defender ever was. This colleague truly despises more reluctant superstars like Barry Bonds, because he isn't skinning and grinning and doing the

Kirby Puckett dance all the time. But that macabre tarantella carries a price. O.J., man, what a guy!, thinks the author. O.J. even gave him the epigram of one of his books, talking about character, and how it was the only thing that really mattered. Well, the only reason O.J. said that was he knew it would impress some sucker.

How would O.J. know of personal character, except via lip service? He was good at recalling the names of executive's children, and that, along with recounting tales of his sexual exploits, took him a long way. I could tell you stories about him that would curl your hair . . . or uncurl it, as the case may be. But who ever wanted to hear anything that questioned the authenticity of O.J.'s character? So my colleague was grievously disappointed and wounded after the double-murder charge, and angry after the verdict.

And who was he angry with? O.J.? No. Me! And people like me. He's the one who got fooled, but it was my fault.

But people—mostly these were black people—knew something was not right with O.J., for a long time before the gruesome double-murder on Bundy Drive in Brentwood in 1994.

White people were confused and let down (this seems to be the underlying theme of the doc), because white people had decided that O.J. Simpson was a "unifying symbol of all races." Black people didn't decide that. Black people didn't think that up. Black people didn't even believe that. Who was he unifying, and to what end?

Black people thought he was one hell of a running back, right up there with Jim Brown maybe. *As a running back.* No more. He never showed anything more. He never tried to. White people never noticed that, because the Juice did prove something to them. He proved he wanted to be like them, kind of, with them, tacitly felt the same way about black people as they did. Tacitly, he *despised* black people. He didn't want them around. He proved this all the way up until he committed a crime, a crime of privilege, and then got off for it. The getting-off part is pretty much beyond the experience of black people in America. But still, somehow, it's the black part that gets the blame. The doc seems unaware of this.

The documentary starts with a flawed premise: that O.J. Simpson was a "unifying symbol for all races." No, he wasn't. Sure, he went to USC, but outside of the football team, what did that have to do with black people? That soothed white people. And yes, he had no comment on the proposed boycott of the 1968 Olympics, but what did that have to do with black people? That soothed white people. Okay, he became a spokesman for Hertz, but, as the doc makes clear, what did that have to do with black people? Byron Lewis of Uniworld and former Hertz exec Jerry Burgdoerfer make it plain that Hertz was trying to reach, not black people, but white people, the business traveler. The director of the Hertz commercials makes it clear there was to be no interaction between Go, O.J., Go, and black people in those commercials, whatsoever, for any reason. Hertz wanted no "guilt" by association. But Juice had absolution.

Even after the double-murder, O.J. was treated not like a black person. I never heard of a black man being charged with a double murder having the handcuffs taken *off* him, and being set free, and being told he could turn himself in next Tuesday, or the Friday after Thanksgiving, or whatever. I never heard of a black man being in a 30-mph freeway "car chase." I never heard of a black man who could have and probably should have gone to trial in the wealthy, nearly all-white enclave where the crime happened, Brentwood—or at least in Santa Monica—suddenly having his trial venue changed to downtown Los Angeles, the homecourt of one of the best trial lawyers in the business, who happened to be black, and where the jury pool would have many more potential jurors of color (the better to be blamed for the Not Guilty verdict, which, on the face of the evidence presented in court, was totally inevitable).

It wasn't black people who hid bloody evidence (assuming there was any bloody evidence) for their old college chum. They would have stood out in Brentwood. It wasn't black people who retained attorney Robert Shapiro on Simpson's behalf. Black people don't run around with the president of King World. And it wasn't black people who recommended attorney Johnnie Cochran to Juice. It wasn't black people who assigned near-incompetent Chris Darden to be a prosecutor, when he couldn't mount a decently damning line of questioning . . . such as, "Mr. Simpson, have you ever stayed at that airport hotel in Chicago before. Why now, this night, after the murders? Aren't you the favored son of the head of a hotel chain, Mr. Simpson. Don't you *always* stay at the Ritz-Carlton Hotel in Chicago, Mr Simpson? Why are you sweating all of a sudden, Mr. Simpson?"

And it surely wasn't black people who hinged the prosecution case on the testimony of Mark Fuhrman, who diddled with evidence and could so easily and legitimately be portrayed as a racist cop. (Fuhrman was so smart, compared to the "niggers" he so despises, that one day, he may go on and discover the antidote for penicillin.)

Don't kid yourself. If white people, the big movers and shakers, had really wanted O.J. Simpson convicted, then he would have been. But he wasn't. So, his was a crime of privilege.

Don't be hauling him back over here with the unprivileged now, tacitly blaming black people in the country who didn't know if Juice did it or not, only that their uncle or brother or son was once railroaded and looked like him. Don't show a roomful of law students cheering a verdict and say they are not cheering Johnnie Cochran. Bernie Goldberg comes close here, when he says the cheering black people were cheering not O.J., but that the system took it right between the eyes. Close, but no cigar. Consciously or not, they were cheering Johnnie Cochran, for winning the legal exercise.

The documentary does slip in some points. You just need to be able to translate them. This doc needs a lot of social subtitles.

Harry Edwards says, "His sentiments were, 'I'm not black, I'm O.J.'" (Those sentiments were echoed, not by blacks, but whites.)

The doc quickly brings Juice up from Louisiana roots through his delinquent teenage years, through his junior college football exploits, to his arrival at conservative, private, bone-white (except for clean-shaven football players) USC.

Juice was always cunning. He saw what few black people were privileged to see at the time. He saw the Network, the Chamber, how USC grads could hook him up with Hertz, the movies, TV, the Ritz-Carlton, the willowy blonde women, anything he wanted.

Black people followed his endeavors on the gridiron in '67 and '68. He was a nice diversion from all of the political assassinations. I was about to enter high school and our school colors were maroon and gold. We ran the I formation like USC and we were in Tennessee, for God's sake, where at the time the state university and all like them in that region had no black players. Zero. So Juice was admired *as an athlete*, for that 64-yard-run against UCLA. That run, and the run for the 2003-yard season at Shea Stadium six years later as a Buffalo Bill, were the high points of his life, as far as black people were concerned. When the high point of your life comes as a junior in college . . . not good. While I admired him, in an off-handed way, I admired SC's Earl McCollough, the Wild Bunch, or QB Jimmy Jones as much.

HBO: "His success had special meaning for black Americans."

On the football field, yes, it did. In the boardrooms, no, it didn't. The documentary should say that. But it seems difficult for it to admit, maybe because it really doesn't appear to *know* that.

In the later '70s, I worked with a young white man from Buffalo in the newspaper business out in Cali. He told me one day that in a bar in Buffalo he had heard Juice tell a willowy young blonde, "Hey baby, s— my c—." I was naive then and blew it off, saying, "We don't talk like that." I figured Juice had more game than that.

We? Little did I know, then.

I met Juice later. We worked on the same set of NBC's "NFL Live" in 1989. That's where I got to know him. You don't need all the gory details here. He played a little game for the bosses, involving stories of sexual exploits, titty bars, and what not. Part of his role was to belittle—if not outright destroy—any other so-called black person in the vicinity. Even back then, Jim Brown told me, "You better watch him, Wiley. That m—f—'s *dangerous.*"

The HBO doc purports that O.J. opened all these doors in TV and cinema. No, he didn't. If it had been up to Juice, nobody would have gone through those doors except him. Jim Brown, Woody Strode, Michael Warren opened doors. Jim had already been a movie star. His filmography comes up short when compared to Denzel Washington's, but with *The Dirty Dozen, Ice Station Zebra,* and *100 Rifles* alone, he did way more than Juice.

Juice's great role was bamboozling white folks. And himself. He began to "buy the hype," as Harry Edwards said, meaning he thought he had a divine right, divine privileges. Once, one of his producers told me he said he thought he was the son of God. I'd tried to throw Juice a rope. "Well, we're all children of God," I said. "No," said the producer. "He said *the* son of God."

Juice felt life was his, and by divine right, divining right down to taking the life of whoever made him feel ridiculous, like a cuckold.

Oh, by the way, Lee Bailey, Dr. Sam Shepard's lawyer, was referred to Simpson's case. And it wasn't a black person who referred him.

So you can see why it seems disingenuous to me to call the doc a Study in Black and White, and then watch as it studies mostly how black people somehow are to blame or should carry guilt for this mess, that this evil is somehow inherent in them.

Like it or not, this is part—and the worst part—of the doc's inference. The doc states that 70 percent of black people thought O.J. was innocent, and 70 percent of white people thought he was guilty. All I know is, I didn't get polled. Amiri Baraka didn't get polled. You can't get any blacker than Baraka, and yet, he said, when asked (and not by white people), "I *know* the bastard did it." Didn't see that on *60 Minutes*, did you? Mr. T must not have been polled. In his Clubber Lang persona, he told Juice he should 'fess up . . . like he would, or something. Jim Brown wasn't polled. Neither were a great many others who weren't shown. The doc doesn't portray this ambiguity, preferring to take the easy percentile way out.

One hoped the documentary would be above the simple pandering of the national media, which ran with handhelds to know-nothings in places like the Bronx or D.C., thousands of miles from the trial and O.J., and asked, "Say, do you think O.J.

did it?" What do you expect to hear from these people? They were not informed about the case. They had no clue, other than historical precedent.

In fact, only the people in the courtroom heard all the evidence. I just happened to hear it all, because I went out to assist Johnnie Cochran in the writing of a book immediately after the trial.

Was JC aware of my experiences with O.J.? Yes. I had detailed them in a book called *Dark Witness*. Cochran still hired me.

He couldn't help it. Not after I pitched him. I told him, compared to him, old Atticus Finch had a day at the beach. It's one thing to uphold the nobility of your profession and its basic tenet that every person deserves the finest representation that can be mounted in his or her defense for an innocent black man in the Deep South of the 1950s who is wrongly accused of murder, while knowing he will never be judged innocent in a court of law, no matter what you do. It's quite another thing to uphold the basic tenet of your profession for a black man who is guilty of *something*, and then have the skill, facility, and wherewithal to do your job and get him off in what had become the racial cauldron of mid-'90s Los Angeles.

A defense attorney's job is "not guilty." Period. Moral judgments are for editorialists, not lawyers. But apparently white Americans can't go there. They can't admit that the defense attorneys were better than the prosecution, kicked their royal butts, and won the intellectual exercise on its face. No. So we're back to Square One.

We've socially retrenched, thanks to a so-called "unifying symbol."

The most trenchant observation (including a few wobbles) of the documentary—despite my protests and opposing views, there are some trenchant observations within the doc—is made by Lawrence Grossberg, professor of Cultural Studies at the University of North Carolina. ". . . . O.J. is a kind of symbolic moment in the history of race relations in America. I think a lot of white Americans didn't believe in affirmative action and they didn't believe in integration and they didn't believe in the welfare state . . . they didn't believe that black people were equal to white people. But they couldn't say it. They couldn't say it without being accused of being a racist. And O.J. gave them the ability, the trial gave them the ability, to say it. So in that sense . . . it fulfilled a moment in history that was already there."

I couldn't agree more. The murder itself was a common crime of passion. So The Trial of O.J. Simpson, the Schism in Black and White, was utterly convenient. Not for black people. It allowed white Americans to express emotions already held, to help make liberal or progressive politics into dirty, fearsome, obscene words.

Hitler would've been fascinated by the The Trial of O.J. Simpson, too. He would've had Leni Reinfenstahl make propaganda of it. To wit:

Mary Jo Kane, a sport sociologist at the University of Minnesota said, "Up until that point [Simpson] had been accepted in white American's homes like no other black athlete had ever been accepted. So one could make the argument that he was one of us, quote unquote . . . . The minute he gets into a jam of his own making, what does he do? He falls back on the race card. So you really aren't one of us when it gets down to it, you are one of them."

Them? What them? Why? Because of a heinous crime of passion murder he tried to beat? I think that makes him a Kennedy. I think it makes him a Skakel. I think it makes him one of us. *All* of us.

The crime itself had no racial component. During the months of the trial, I kept clippings of crimes similar to the murders of Nicole Brown Simpson and the unfortunate Ron Goldman, mostly committed by men, often spouses, against women, often their wives. I stopped after three months. Why? I was running out of storage space.

These crimes of passion happen every day. They know no color.

So who or what made it about color? Was it Simpson? Was it the fascination, then disappointment, whites had in him? Was it Mark Fuhrman? Lee Bailey? Johnnie Cochran? Media? Documentaries?

To paraphrase Humphrey Bogart in *Casablanca*: Of all the innocent black men who rotted in jails or swung from trees for "crimes" they didn't commit all over the landscape through this bloody century and the entire history of the country, out of all those doomed, forgotten people, *this* is the guy who gets off?

Surely this is the most terrible irony of my lifetime. And one day, maybe, someone will examine it *all*, thoroughly, clinically and clearly, in a documentary film.

Apparently, that day is not yet here.

—ESPN.com, November 13, 2002

JOHN THOMPSON

Throughout his career few subjects intimidated Wiley, but John Thompson was one of them. As Wiley saw it in 1991, the famed coach of Georgetown University's basketball team was inspiring, wise, outspoken, and unapologetic. In other words, a great teacher.

I was anxious to meet John Thompson. I hadn't felt such unilateral confusion, open dislike, heated rancor, unswerving loyalty, and good faith toward a black man in American athletics since the days of Muhammad Ali. America told a lot about itself through John Thompson, so I figured this must be a man worth knowing. At the same time, I didn't feel I would get to know the essence of Thompson. I would know no more than what he ever lets the world know. He feels it is enough for us to know he can coach the game, coach all the false air and pride out of it, and reduce it to its essentials.

It was enough we knew he would win seven times out of ten. John Thompson had proven it while coaching the basketball team at Georgetown University. He and his teams had given college basketball history three of its greatest championship games. His teams lost two of those three games, by a total of three points. Even this didn't mellow the general public's attitude toward Thompson. He also won one of the games. This was too great or small a percentage. Thompson seemed to touch people inside, like Muhammad Ali, and I hoped he could reveal to me how he accomplished this, since it seemed to be satisfying and profitable work.

Thompson is a six-foot-ten-inch man of imposing physical proportions, but surprisingly lithe, with a gracefulness undeniable in his movements, especially when he strode on and off the court before a Georgetown game. A big man, as always, but somehow smaller than he is always pictured until you glance at that massive head and the sadness naturally constructed around his eyes. If his expression is blank, he looks precisely as though something is troubling him.

Thompson had been educated in the cream of white institutions—John Carroll High School in Washington; Providence College; the Boston Celtics; coach at St. Anthony's, another Catholic high school; and finally as coach for the team at the Jesuit university. When he was in elementary school, the story went, Thompson had been tested and found not to have high intelligence. This was only the beginning of the insults, which would always occur no matter how well-meaning people were. There was no way for a man the size and complexion of Thompson to hide from this, so he decided not to try.

Whatever Thompson became as he reached forty-six, he had white institutions to thank for it, at least in part. He'd known rejection, so when his time came he carried no guilt for doing his own rejecting. He rejected any notion that he had to explain his actions to the national media or anybody else. He was civilized. He did his job supremely. This was his reply, his revenge of living well.

He liked to be seen as a serious, taciturn sort, gruff even, as I found on our first meeting, which came in 1984. Then I was there to see Patrick Ewing, the seven-foot center who was thought to be the personification of Thompson on the court. The second time I met Thompson, two years later, he was still playing gruff. Again, I was not there to see him, *per se*, but Reggie Williams, another Georgetown All-American player. It was still Thompson I wished to know.

But John tests you first. He tells you he doesn't have the time or inclination for you. Just as he was once told, at face value, by voice, thought, action, and innuendo. And he had to overcome that, survive that, make people see him through that lens. So he merely asks the same of you. If you become insulted by his lack of care, and then leave in a huff, and resent him, well, then he has done what he wished to do. He has made you feel as he felt. If you stay with it, eventually he gives you what you need. I stayed with it.

The third time I met Thompson, we spoke at length, and pleasantly. He spoke earnestly, even though we never did shake hands at those meetings. How one could test his intelligence and find it lacking was beyond me. The man was a fountain of ideas, theories, thoughts, anecdotes. I asked him what he made of people saying he was intimidating.

"I try not to spend too much time evaluating or defending John Thompson. It's more important to me to do that which I feel is correct. I leave the rest to other people. It's been my experience that people, regardless of being white or black, have come to me and told me they didn't like something I said, or commended me on something I said. I don't think John Thompson can ever say the thing or do the thing that will win all the people over. Christ came down here and couldn't do that. I don't expect John Thompson to do that. The most important thing for me is to be as honest as I can and to reveal the truth as I perceive it. I can't worry for instance if a member of the media comes in and has a negative experience with me and then tries to define me.

"I've been with me for forty-six years and can't define me. It's impossible for someone to come in and have one experience with me and declare, 'This is who John Thompson is.' I'd like to think I'm more complicated than one meeting."

When I asked Thompson about some white people who had questions about how many white players he would have on the U.S. Olympic team in 1988, he smiled and said:

"I personally feel that when you ask a black person that question, it is intended to make the victim the criminal. That's a very tactless question. What it implies is that I am committing a criminal act against someone else, and it is very misleading. To my knowledge, black people never held anyone in slavery in this country. The question is used to turn that part of your life around in which you were the victim, making you appear to be the person who committed the crime. The crime was committed against black folks. So I don't feel the need to explain to anybody what the racial makeup of my team will be. I feel I'm fair enough as an individual to know those people, regardless of who is white or black, best capable of bringing home the Olympic gold medal to the United States. Although it would be a lot easier if I had Patrick Ewing and Michael Jordan. I do feel those questions are ploys to turn your role in society around.

"That's what I feel. I will not have a quota. No one picks my team or gives me quotas. Nobody has ever gone to my son and asked him how he feels to be the only black player on the Princeton basketball team. I refuse to be manipulated."

Thompson's team at Georgetown was black by majority. If a white player had the nerve to come out for the team and stay out, Thompson might just keep him. Not if he was weak-minded, though. I had heard stories where recruiters from other colleges would make sure that any white player talented enough to really play for Georgetown would never consider it. The recruiters accomplished this by saying, "Oh, you don't want to go *there*." Thompson was not angered by this. He was a tactician. He admired tactics. He would put a team on the floor. He'd win with what he had.

What Thompson had were kids of all different classes. Unfortunately, class has become synonymous with money. This has been an unworthy fate for class. To me, class has to do with choice, taste, carriage, grooming, manner, and the like. But household income, holdings, and inheritances determine class in America. By my own measure, if a young man was not at least middle class when he came to Georgetown to play for John Thompson—and a few of them who did already were—then he surely would be by the time Thompson got through with him. Anytime Georgetown's teams traveled, they were impeccably dressed, carried themselves ramrod-straight and kept noise down. They lived with the school's general population in the dormitories. They were not a band of physically gifted ragamuffins there to perform a minstrel show for free. They were there to do business.

What Thompson's teams demonstrated, above all, was a certain discipline. No need to wonder about this discipline's origin. I felt this made some uneasy. Power can be so vain it believes there can be no order unless power brings order. Without power, there can only be chaos. Thompson verified this as myth, even as his teams were labeled desperately chaotic by powers that be. Order brings power. If a young man spent four years at Georgetown, he left with class.

Inevitably, all of this only helped the public marketing of John Thompson and college basketball. He liked to say, "I don't care what people think. As long as they come inside." Thompson was easy for white people to embrace as a villain, I felt. It took no thought for them to dislike him. He was as black as Darth Vader, or Black Monday or devil's food cake or any other of those negative metaphors so popular in our time. And his teams were always, always excellent. Even in his down years he'd somehow win twenty, and a victory over Georgetown was celebrated with a special verve. Like Ali and Darth Vader before him, Thompson sold tickets.

He also made white people see themselves more clearly in relation to their own assumptions of liberalism. When the Georgetown team was involved in the occasional on-court fight or brawl, Georgetown basketball was called violent, and Georgetown basketball was John Thompson. After the 1988 season, a rule against brawls came into college basketball. The Georgetown rule. People had even made claims that the Georgetown teams were the only ones ever involved in fights. This was how ridiculous it became. Meanwhile, people would conveniently forget fights like the one between Syracuse and Providence in the Final Four in 1987, or by Yale and Dartmouth any year.

These incidents were forgotten, even later remembered fondly, as they should have been, for in fact sometimes in the heat of competition these things will happen. Boys will be boys. One presumed writer in a New York newspaper, whose dislike of Thompson apparently knew only distant bounds, wrote that the fact Thompson's players usually graduated and stayed out of drug rehab and went on to do positive things was not the point. The writer said the point was that of the last ten fights on a basketball court he had seen, Georgetown had been involved in all of them.

Apparently the writer closed his eyes any time other teams scuffled on the court. To say this scuffling was the point of anything was doubly racist. In the first place, the writer must have believed the only thing black people were cut out to do was play basketball, if getting into a scuffle on the court was more important than becoming a judge. And it was flagrantly racist to deny that other teams scuffle.

In fact, most of the scuffles involving Georgetown came because, like Thompson himself, his Hoyas rarely backed down. In most cases, the Hoyas played the game better than the teams they faced. The Hoyas were coached better. When being bested, a player does whatever is necessary to remain competitive. Such is the nature of competition in some. Some will elbow, shove, scratch, reach, talk about your mother, and anything else, because playing pure basketball against a John Thompson team was to invite defeat. Thompson's teams played for forty minutes, ninety-four feet, end line to end line, and had been taught the details of man-to-man defense by one of the great masters. So when confronted by the tactics of survival against the unrelenting pressure, the Hoyas didn't back off.

What is rarely underscored about Thompson is that he takes his defeats so well. He was congratulatory toward the Villanova coach, Rollie Massimino, much as he had been toward Dean Smith, whose North Carolina team, led by Michael Jordan, beat Georgetown in the championship game in 1982, probably the greatest championship game ever played. When a Georgetown player, Fred Brown, threw the ball to a North Carolina player, James Worthy, by mistake in the final seconds, Thompson embraced Brown on the court.

A year after the 1985 Georgetown-Villanova championship game, it came out that Gary McLain, the Villanova point guard, was taking cocaine all through the week of the championship game. Thompson was such a strong father figure that his players rarely if ever succumbed to such behavior while in college. If they had, he would have known it and it would not have been tolerated. Another player, Len Bias, expired on the campus of the University of Maryland while using cocaine. This part of Thompson's teaching process and prowess was rarely examined, because it went against the villainous image, which was so easy and profitable.

Meanwhile, black people not directly involved seemed just as unanimous in their support and outright love for Thompson as white people were in their dislike. All of this made for great American theater and a tremendous profit, not only for television and the NCAA, but also for Georgetown and John Thompson. "I'd like to be remembered as a teacher," Thompson said. "And I'd like to be rich. I stress to my young men that we are in a capitalistic system where the object is gain for work done." To that end, Georgetown hung the professional NBA jerseys of its basketball graduates in McDonough Arena, the home of the Hoyas, on the Washington, D.C., campus of the great Jesuit university where a black man was a loud, difficult, and ultimately beneficent king.

"Well, I haven't spent a lot of time thinking about how people perceive me. I am six-foot-ten-inches, I'm black, I'm loud. If you see a big tree in the forest that has large roots, it makes an impression on you. I have large hands, large mouth, make big sounds. Even if I'm not angry, I am loud, and saying what you feel, some people are going to perceive that as intimidating. I cannot control what a person perceives. I know what my intentions are. I feel it is important to say the things I feel to be correct. I don't intentionally try to hurt anybody's feelings or to intimidate anybody, unless I feel they are trying to offend me purposely. It is important to me to express what I perceive as the truth. Sometimes I'm incorrect. I didn't want to go through this experience called education, just to be perceived as a good person. I have to say the truth. The public is more important than the press.

"I don't think of it as making a stand for myself. I just do what comes naturally to me. When I was attending John Carroll High, a person sat up and taught history, philosophy, mathematics. There was no white math or black math. He teaches also justice. What's right and wrong. If you sit in that classroom, and learn these things, why when you see an injustice, you don't think about whether it's white or black. I'm a product of the society that educated me. I was not educated to distinguish that this set of rules go for white people and these for blacks. I don't care where you've been educated. If you came through the American system, you've had experiences which have been degrading if you are an American black man. And I think you don't hold anybody responsible, but I think you are bound to make society aware these things exist when you see they exist."

There was little doubt, in my mind at least, that John Thompson, Dean Smith of North Carolina, and Bobby Knight of Indiana were the best college coaches of their time and fairly responsible, for better or worse, for the explosion of college basketball as a televised entertainment entity. Thompson and Knight were considered ogres by some, but Knight had much, much more rope.

If Thompson had thrown a chair across a court or taken his team off the court and quit cold in a game against the Russians or snatched players by their jerseys during games or, no matter how innocently, talked about relaxing while enjoying rape—my God, you can imagine the reaction. John Thompson would have been run out of town. That was my assumption. But if Thompson had done things of that nature, they would have been calculated. He would have survived. Thompson seemed to do nothing without a reason. He was very controlled and seemed to live a very structured life. There was very little wasted motion of any kind in his daily schedule, and he didn't spend time bowing to social conventions, other than the manners his parents had bestowed on him. His bark was much more severe than his bite.

Thompson was going to win seven times out of ten as surely as the sun was going to rise the next day. So the continuum of the public reaction to him was assured, as was the continuation of Georgetown basketball and the final realization of his desire to become rich. The irony is this: My given was that white people removed from Thompson nearly unanimously despised him, either secretly or out loud, but always wished him the best, always figured he was right, and wanted his team to be the best.

But Thompson felt that white people close to Georgetown were his most solid allies. "It is my own people, black people, who try to do us harm from close," he said. I must admit that after considering it, this illumination did not exactly stun me.

I told him, or rather I suggested to him, that surely he was aware that this was not uncommon. Thompson allowed that. This manifestation of self-hatred was not directed at him, or his terrible burden to bear alone, warping only his judgment, but was a binding generality. He also made it plain that he would be sabotaged for no one. Not even for old times' sake. Not even if some things changed.

John Thompson was able to extract the essence of most American people, make us all so obvious and translucent to one another, if only we would pay attention to ourselves and our visceral reactions to this one man. Thompson had convinced himself few of us mattered to him because he didn't like what he saw when he pulled out the essence of his fellow men. What he did find seemed to motivate him.

This is why Thompson assumed nothing about people, went so far, was so vilified, so honored, so respected, and even, in a strange way, was needed by Americans, much as people later found they loved and respected Muhammad Ali. Thompson was just a coach, just a teacher, in fact one of the few teachers paid an appropriate scale in this society of wasted motions and vain ideas of class. I knew that somewhere out there an impatient boy or girl was watching, listening to the drum, waiting for a chance to do what Thompson does, only better. In the end, this is what made Thompson just as valuable an icon in his time as Ali had been in his.

Black people knew they could fight and scuffle, and be proud of their independence. What Thompson demonstrated was how well black people can teach. Maybe he'd make teaching unpopular. Maybe that was too much to ask of us. Unfortunately, I've never been to a basketball game where a seminar broke out unless Georgetown was involved.

—*From Why Black People Tend to Shout, 1991*

WHY DID
DURAN DO IT?

With sixteen seconds left in the eighth round of his November 1980 title fight with Sugar Ray Leonard, the great Roberto Duran held up his gloves and told the referee, "No mas, no mas." That the previously invincible Duran had quit astonished not only Leonard, but also fans and sportswriters around the world. But Wiley had a theory: Maybe the fighter had seen who his next opponent would have to be, Thomas "Hit Man" Hearns.

Roberto Duran is smarter than any of them gave him credit for. He got his way, and he will get his money. Some say fix. Whenever your man loses, fix is the easy way out. But I have no doubt that Duran intended to knock Ray Leonard's head off his shoulders when the fight began. After all, he is Roberto Duran.

But what Duran found in the ring sobered him. Leonard was fighting hard and impeccably. He was popping in that jab, and Duran could counter it only one time out of seven. To make matters worse, Leonard was getting the best of it inside. Roberto found Ray, but was found himself even more often. And Leonard was not breathing hard.

Duran did not want to be embarrassed, as he was in the seventh round, by a man he still does not respect as a fistfighter, so he threw up his hands and robbed Leonard of his satisfaction. That was just like Duran.

Some say, "Well, Ali went thirteen rounds with a broken jaw," and then puff up as if they did this themselves. I say Duran is smarter. He could see the handwriting on *The Wall Street Journal*. He didn't want to go out sitting in his corner with two black eyes. Yeah, he quit, and anybody who wants to call him a coward is welcome to go down to Panama and tell him themselves. Duran will be there.

Then again, perhaps Duran gave up the ghost because he caught a glimpse of the tall, slenderish man with dispassionate eyes dressed in a cranberry suit. That would be Thomas Hearns, and Duran would have been a mark for him. Thomas Hearns is the legacy, another kiss that Duran blows to Leonard.

"I'm here to dominate this division," said the king of Detroit. "I want the winner. Duran, the little short man, he's a midget, there's no way he could have beat me anyway. Sugar Ray? I really don't believe he's got the heart."

Hearns could steal the heart of the greatest welterweights. He is a physical strangeling, a 147-pounder who stands on ostrich legs with a heavyweight's reach and thunder in both hands. But you all know that by now. What you don't know is how Hearns would fight Ray Leonard. Listen.

"Our basic strategy against Ray would be to change up, to keep him off balance, box him," said Emanuel Steward, the trainer.

"I can't see no man 5-10 out-jabbing Tommy," said Steward, answering an Angelo Dundee charge that Leonard's jab would get there first. "They talk about Tommy's chin. I've watched him for twelve years, against Poles and Russians and Cubans. He's never been knocked down. One of his strongest assets is his chin.

"I have more headaches worrying about Wilfred Benitez than the others. He's hungry. He lost the title, and now he sees those big purses. It's a fight that Thomas needs."

Thomas says, "I'm not even thinking about Benitez. He would be no problem for me. He's the farthest thing from my mind." (They fight in January.)

Athletes have gotten better in every other sport, but I'm not so sure about boxing. Oh, I think the welterweights are as good now as they've ever been, from a strictly physical standpoint, but attitudes are different.

The promoters have no one to blame but themselves. In the old days, a title fight would be worth $25 or $30,000. Any champ worth his salt would run through that kind of money in no time, and be hungry for more. Now, with millions as a payday, the fighter has no reason to fight.

Thomas Hearns is a throwback to those days, mentally. Already he is building a mental animosity toward Ray Leonard. He wants Leonard bad.

Leonard is like Ali. Leonard has great physical skills. He still has the fastest hands in the division, and even Steward admits that he has a rock for a chin. But like Ali, Leonard wants to win and be paid. He doesn't necessarily want to fight. He does not enjoy being hit. He would rather pull his head back out of the way and avoid that, and I for one cannot find anything wrong with this evolution among great fighters. It will be less men slobbering on themselves in later life.

Hearns comes to fight, to destroy. He is still very hungry, for blood and money. As I say, Leonard has great skills, enough skills to make a fight of it. If both were angry and panged with hunger, they could stage one of the greatest fights of any era. But, attitudes being what they are, Hearns would kill Ray Leonard and only be sorry about it after the fact.

If Leonard is smart, he'll walk away, too.

—The Oakland Tribune, November 27, 1980

THE UNDERTAKER
WAS BURIED

Despite Wiley's original prediction that Sugar Ray Leonard would be wise not fight Thomas Hearns, when the two men finally stepped into the ring in 1981, it was Leonard who walked out victorious. Still, as this Oakland Tribune *column makes clear: there was plenty of praise to go around for two true warriors.*

The survivalists would hate Sugar Ray Leonard. The survivalists are those folk who have given up on civilization. They have run from the face of doom. They are fearful, nervous, afraid. They are not Ray Leonard's kind of people, obviously.

Thomas Hearns was the face of doom. In a one-to-one confrontation he was—is—as frightening as any bomb. But Leonard defused the bomb Wednesday night. He fought the fight of the master boxer who does what he must do. He fought Hearns with one eye. Hearns's left hand had closed the other. But, at the darkest hour, Leonard turned doom in on itself. He showed Thomas Hearns a mirror. Hearns was maneuvered into fighting Leonard's fight, and no mortal man can do that and stand for long.

That is now a point of historical fact. Two Sugars, please.

There was only a small window for Leonard to come through in this fight. That was evident in the first two rounds, when Leonard chose to circle and evade while Hearns, confident, held the middle ring. There was no way Leonard could win rounds from the perimeter, and he had lost those two.

The Room is a term borrowed from Muhammad Ali, who likened being hit into a state of semi-consciousness to being in a dark room, surrounded by, among other things, bats blowing saxophones. In the sixth round, Leonard sent Hearns to the Carlsbad Cavern Jazz Festival, in stereo.

Here is where Hearns proved his worth. Here is where he was knocked into the ropes, buckling and unaware. But he fought through the smoke. He came back to hurt Leonard. But the point had been made, and Thomas Hearns was a changed fighter after that. He did not like that Room. No air there.

So, from then on, Hearns fought from his toes, and Leonard stalked the center of the ring. Yes, Hearns proved from there until the fourteenth that indeed he could box, feint, and combinate. But he was on his toes. He was jabbing. He was exhorting the crowd. He was trying to be sweet, and he lost his power.

Meanwhile, Leonard's left hook was whittling Hearns's body, while Hearns was content to jab Leonard's swelling left eye. But Leonard's body attack pulled Hearns's arms down. And Hearns's blows, so telling early when he was putting body behind them, became mere flicks. He did not want to return to that Room. He stopped punching. He started jabbing, backing up.

The only question was, would Ray catch up before time ran out? He stayed in Hearns's face, so the tall man could not extend. The mutual respect now belonged mostly to Leonard. Hearns was doing the running.

Hearns won the tenth, eleventh, and twelfth, off the jab and his toes. It was the worst thing that could have happened to him. He came out in the thirteenth, and his whole being was directed toward Leonard's eye. He forgot his own.

It was a simple one-two that did it. Left-right, and Hearns was his. Leonard pounded Hearns through the ropes. The champion's face was a horrible mask of swollen eye and raging determination. He buried Hearns through the ropes near Hearns's corner. Hearns got up shaking his head, saying no, but Leonard's accumulated fury drove him back down again.

In the fourteenth, it was just a matter of finding the spot. Leonard hit Hearns flush with the right, again near Hearns's corner. Hearns was in the Room to stay. He did not go down, but he was out.

It was everything they said it would be.

When Hearns left the ring, he was unsteady, still feeling his way back into our world, the one we take for granted. In the ring, not even the shut eye could dull the luster of Ray Leonard's smile.

"That was a dull fight, a lousy fight," a sportswriter said to me as we entered the interview area. I had no patience. I found myself saying, "Well, what did you want? Death?"

No, not death, just a rematch. Ray did not want to ponder on such matters Wednesday night, and who can blame him? He had just nuked the nuker. He had just cancelled Doomsday. He had just turned in the fight of his life, in terms of tactics, strength, ability, intelligence, and heart. He had just buried the Undertaker, and there was no need to resurrect him, not just yet. At least let the eye stop hurting.

"I take my hat off to Mr. Hearns," said Leonard. "I don't have much to say [regarding a rematch] I have just proven myself as the greatest welterweight in the world. But I say, in my book, we both are still champions."

A Hearns bettor crumpled his marker and, near tears, said, "And he was giving him a boxing lesson, too. Thomas was actually showing Ray how to box."

That was the problem. Nobody shows Ray Leonard how to box, and you can take that to the Room, and the bank.

—The Oakland Tribune, September 17, 1981

THEN ALL THE JOY
TURNED TO SORROW

Several days before his 1982 title fight with world lightweight champion Ray "Boom Boom" Mancini, challenger Duk Koo Kim wrote a prophetic message on a lampshade in his hotel room: Kill or Be Killed. *The fight with Mancini was furious, lasting fourteen rounds, and when it was over, Kim collapsed into a coma and was rushed to the hospital. Following the fight, Wiley wrote this* Sports Illustrated *cover story, and shortly after it went to press, Duk Koo Kim died.*

Ray "Boom Boom" Mancini held his swollen left hand in front of him like a jewel while shading his battered brow with his right. The bright lights were harsh and unwelcome. There were questions in Mancini's heart about what had just happened in the ring, though he didn't yet know the full horror of what had occurred. Was the WBA lightweight title he had just defended successfully against South Korea's Duk Koo Kim worth this? Was anything? "Why do I do it?" Mancini asked himself. "Why do I do this? I'm the one who has to wake up tomorrow and look at myself." He fingered the purple, misshapen area around his left eye. "A badge of honor," he said in a morbid tone. Minutes earlier, a less reflective Mancini had scored a technical knockout of Kim nineteen seconds into the fourteenth round, and Kim had been carried from the outdoor ring at Caesars Palace in Las Vegas on a stretcher. This was to have been an epilogue to the Aaron Pryor-Alexis Arguello WBA junior welterweight title fight the night before. Tragically, it became a nightmare.

The twenty-three-year-old Kim, who rained an incredible number of blows on Mancini and in return was pounded by even more, was injured by two right hands his head could not bear. Kim was taking just four breaths per minute when he was transported from the ring to an ambulance that was destined for Desert Springs Hospital.

Kim then underwent two-and-a-half hours of brain surgery, performed by Dr. Lonnie Hammargren, a local neurosurgeon, who removed a 100-cc. blood clot from the right side of Kim's brain. The clot, Dr. Hammargren said, was the result of a broken blood vessel and "due, in all probability, to one tremendous punch to the head." Had the punch been part of the thrty-nine-blow bombardment Mancini had delivered in the opening fifty seconds of the thirteenth round? Was it the first of the final two rights in the fourteenth? Or the second? Or could the damage have been done not by Mancini's fists but by Kim's head hitting the canvas after the final blow? Could Kim's brain have been damaged before the fight? "The hemorrhage was quite fresh," the neurosurgeon said on Saturday night. "The trauma was caused by one punch."

Dr. Hammargren had previously performed two similar operations, one on a Japanese kick boxer, the other on another fighter. "Both men wound up normal, but this outcome will be much worse. Mr. Kim had a right subdural hematoma," said Dr. Hammargren two hours after the surgery was completed. "He's very critical, with terminal brain damage. There is severe brain swelling. The pressure will go up and up, and that will be it. He'll die. His pupils have been fixed since he arrived. We have him on the respirator now. His body responds slightly to painful stimulus, and that is the only real sign of life we've had. They tell me he fought like a lion in the thirteenth round. Well, nobody could fight like that with a blood clot on his brain."

As *SI* went to press Monday evening, Kim, who had almost no remaining brain function, was being maintained by a life-support system.

Kim had indeed fought like a lion. Through the thirty-nine minutes of the previous rounds and those final nineteen seconds, the crowd of 6,500 at Caesars was sated with action, as was a CBS television audience. And everyone, especially co-promoter Bob Arum, seemed pleased when the fight was over. But later, at the hospital, Arum was somber. "Suspend boxing for a few months," he suggested, and he called for headgear for boxers and more heavily padded gloves. "Get a blue-chip medical panel to investigate this thing first, and then suspend boxing," Arum said. "It is the height of irresponsibility to allow this to happen, and the old excuses are not working."

Back at Caesars, Mancini learned of the severity of Kim's injuries and left his suite in the company of his parents and Father Tim O'Neill, the family priest, to seek refuge elsewhere.

Before the fight, Kim's training methods, which included hammering a tire with a sledgehammer 200 times daily and ingesting large amounts of ginseng and garlic, and his style had not impressed the boxing cognoscenti. His anonymity seemed to diminish his 17-1-1, eight-KO record and his No. 1 ranking by the WBA. But he was to become a haunting foe for Mancini, who now finds, eerily, that he may fight Kim forever, and in doing so, fight himself.

Mancini is five-foot-six, the same as Kim. Mancini fought low. Kim fought lower. Mancini is righthanded, Kim lefthanded. There was a quarter-inch difference in reach, a half-pound in weight, little difference in power, and absolutely none in approach. "It was murderous," said Mancini's manager, Dave Wolf, immediately after the bout, unaware at the time that the comment would soon take on a macabre ring. "It was like Ray was fighting a mirror. I hope the people who said Kim was nothing are impressed now."

Mancini was left with several impressions by the 14th round. In the third, an infrequent Kim right lead—or perhaps it was a clash of heads—ripped open Mancini's left ear. Blood spouted, and only ice and pressure by cornerman Paul Percifield kept the wound closed. In that same round, one of Mancini's left hooks caught Kim's head too high and at a bad angle. The hand, badly bruised by the blow, began to swell, eventually to twice normal size. In the eighth, Mancini's left eye began to puff and color.

Kim's left hooks and slashing rights had exacted a toll, but Kim had been punished, too, though he showed it less. When the fighters began the fourteenth, the mirror's image was still there. Mancini broke the pattern by stepping to the right as Kim's left whistled by. Mancini hooked his own wounded left ineffectually, but now Kim was off-center, exhausted, and facing Mancini's corner. Mancini drove off his right foot and delivered the first of the final pair of rights on the point of the Korean's chin.

A glancing left hook followed, then a crushing right which sent Kim to the canvas. Kim landed heavily on his back and head, rolled over in slow motion, grabbed a middle strand of the ropes and stared blankly at the timekeeper. Kim's eyes dilated while the outdoor stadium rocked in celebration. "He was desperate, and I was hoping. My left hand was killing me," Mancini said. "But I felt that first right all the way up my arm." Twice Kim failed to regain his footing, but somehow he beat the count. Referee Richard Green looked at Kim's unfocused eyes and buckling legs and stopped the fight. "He was not there, and I wasn't going to let him go any further," said Green, who has officiated half a dozen world title fights, including Larry Holmes-Muhammad Ali. Green was absolved of any blame for failing to stop the fight sooner by the attending ringside physician, Dr. Donald Romeo, who worked to revive Kim. Kim's cornermen had offered no protest when the fight ended. "He just wouldn't go down," one of them said. "He had great pride."

Perhaps Kim's pride had been too great. Wolf returned from the hospital eight hours after the fight, at 11 p.m., sobered. "Pol Tiglao [Kim's American representative and translator and agent for a number of Oriental fighters] told me that a couple of days before the fight, Kim had written 'Kill or Be Killed' in Korean on a lampshade in his room," Wolf said. "He was a warrior going to war. Apparently he viewed this as a death match." Wolf then discounted Arum's suggestions. "I don't know what a blue-ribbon panel could do," he said. "It was not a case of defective equipment, or a fighter being allowed to go too far, or any impropriety. It was one or two unfortunate punches. And those rights at the end were not nearly the best punches Ray had thrown during the fight."

The youngest of five children born to rice and ginseng farmers, Kim came from Kang Won-Do province in Korea, 100 kilometers east of Seoul. "He was the strongest of the family's three sons," said H. R. Lee, a Lorean journalist with the *Hankook Ilbo*, who traveled to Las Vegas with Kim's small entourage and a larger group of Korean partisans. "He was not injured before the fight. He was in the best condition of his life."

Kim had been a shoeshine boy, tour guide, and baker's assistant before starting an amateur boxing career in 1976. His only hobby, according to Lee, was "music listening," but Tiglao said he also enjoyed reading. After a 29-4 amateur record, he turned professional in 1978, working with 100 other fighters in Seoul's Tong-a Gymnasium. He was the best of the lot and won the Orient and Pacific Boxing Federation lightweight title last February. He received $20,000 to fight Mancini.

Mancini studied film of Kim and other southpaw fighters for weeks. "We figured he'd come out kamikaze," Mancini said. "After looking at the film, I didn't care what anyone said," Mancini's trainer, Murphy Griffith, declared. "I had Ray train as if it was the fight of his life."

So it was. Mancini started the first round with a booming left hook to the jaw, but Kim answered with two of his own, and the barrages from both sides continued for the first nine rounds, the only variation being target. When Mancini went to the liver or rib cage, Kim answered. Mancini hooked with the hooker and found the tactic somewhat lacking. Kim seemed to land the harder punches. At the end of the ninth, a left rocked Mancini back on his heels, and Kim extended his arms upward in exultation. "He was getting lower than me," Mancini said. "I was supposed to be off him, but a lot of times when a guy is sitting in front of you like that, you want to move in and shoot. But he was getting his punches off first." Said Griffith, "Ray had to adjust. We didn't know Kim would be that tough. He was skillful, smart. Ray couldn't get below him, where he likes to be. But Ray's physical conditioning determined the fight. By the 13th round, the guy was looking for the hook. I told Ray to go with the right."

In fact, that decision had been made some ten rounds earlier, when Mancini hurt his hand. "Every time I hit him in the head, it killed me," Mancini said shortly after the battle, unaware of the terrible irony. The constant pounding from Mancini began to tell on Kim in the tenth, when Green took a point from Kim for hitting-and-holding. Green was berated by Mancini's corner throughout the fight about that tactic, borderline low blows, hitting after the bell, and Kim's headfirst rushes. "He wasn't dirty," insisted Mancini, who appeared to win every round from the tenth on. "Rough and tough, not dirty. We both hit heads. We both hit low. He was just the worst type of guy to fight." Said Wolf, "Already I can look back and see that [Green] did an excellent job."

By the eleventh, though his left eye was purple and hideously swollen, Mancini had taken control of the fight. He fired a left hook that buckled Kim's knees, and now he began to land three punches to Kim's one. At one point Kim went to one knee, but Green correctly ruled it a push. Mancini ended the twelfth scoring from a distance. He gave himself a clap and made an exaggerated nod at the end of the round. In the thirteenth, Mancini swarmed over Kim, starting the unanswered thirty-nine-punch sequence with a straight right hand. The right side of Kim's jaw ballooned and appeared to be broken, but he weathered that storm and even managed to punch out a weak combination. Then came the fourteenth, the sidestep, and Mancini's initial right, apparently unseen by Kim. He reeled back, defenseless, and the second right landed point blank on his jaw.

"Let all these guys who are screaming for a piece of Ray settle with Kim first. A temporary champion would have lost to Kim today," Wolf said at the conclusion of the bout. Later, after spending four hours at the hospital and being told that Kim didn't have long to live, Wolf said, "Ray is taking this hard, and his parents are pretty shook up also. I haven't given a single thought to how this may affect Ray as a fighter, and maybe that sounds silly, but that's the last concern right now. How it affects him as a person is what concerns me. I do think he's a very strong kid and sometime in the future he will be able to look at this, in the context of great pain, and see that once he stepped into that ring with Kim there was nothing he could have done."

On Sunday morning, one hour before attending a mass conducted by Father O'Neill at the Tropicana Hotel, Mancini issued a statement on CBS, which had televised the fight. Dark glasses covering his closed left eye, his damaged hand resting on the arm of the couch in his suite, Mancini said, "I'm very saddened. I'm sorry it had to happen, and it hurts me bad that I was part of it. I hope they realize I didn't intentionally hurt him. I don't blame myself, but I can't alienate myself.

"I'm a Christian, and I've been praying that I'll get some answers to questions that have been popping through my mind," Mancini said softly. "I have to rely on my faith to get me through this. It could easily have been me, and who is to say that it won't be me next time? I'm not saying I'll retire, but right now I'm not thinking of future fights. I have to see what happens to Mr. Kim. I need time to heal."

His was to be one of the last of Mancini's modest purses—his career earnings were pushed over $1 million by a $250,000 guarantee against forty-five percent of the gross revenue from this fight. Howard Davis was a likely springtime opponent. And then, of course, there was Pryor. Arguello, the only man to beat Mancini, is still the WBC lightweight champion. "I had always pictured myself coming back and doing that to Alexis," Mancini had said while viewing Pryor's destruction of Arguello Friday night.

"We'd be interested in Pryor," Wolf said at the time.

Emile Griffith fought 80 times after Benny "Kid" Paret died following their fight on March 24, 1962. Griffith was 24 at the time of the Paret bout, a career fighter comfortably lost in his craft. Is Mancini, still impressionable at 21 and a young man for whom "money is no god," different? "They are both sensitive individuals," said Gil Clancy, CBS boxing analyst and former manager of Griffith, who happens to be the nephew of Mancini's trainer. "It took something out of Emile Griffith," said Clancy. "Griffith got hate mail, but he got encouragement, too. Ray will have to deal with the same things." Murphy Griffith said, "For a while it was doubtful that Emile would ever come back. He was a sensitive man. But time heals. He had to realize that what happened wasn't his will. People say it affected him until the end of his career. I think it did. Man, you don't forget. Some can handle it, some can't. How it will happen in Ray's case, only time will tell. He's got a good head, but a human is a human."

Former heavyweight champion Max Baer never approached a fight with the same intensity following the death of Frankie Campbell soon after their fight in San Francisco on Aug. 24, 1930. Jimmy Doyle died 17 hours after fighting Sugar Ray Robinson for the welterweight crown in Cleveland on June 24, 1947. At a subsequent hearing Robinson was asked whether he knew he had Doyle in serious trouble. "They pay me to get them in trouble," said Robinson.

Mancini's box-office appeal had had nearly everyone who

could make the weight calling him to try to get a fight. Despite his 24-1, nineteen-KO record, Mancini inspired confidence in contenders. Their pre-Las Vegas feelings can be summed up in the words of Hector Camacho, an undefeated junior lightweight from New York's Spanish Harlem. "You can't play Mancini cheap, he's the man right now," Camacho had said the night before the Mancini-Kim fight. "He's strong, he'll beat on you, but when the time comes he won't knock me out. He's the guy that will make me. He will make me. He's good, but he don't have that, you know, that greatness."

"Look, I know people either think I'm a bum or a superstar," Mancini had said. "I don't care what they think. I know where I am. Somewhere in between." Later, just before he'd heard the news of Kim's condition, Mancini decided something. "This badge of honor," he said, studying his face in the mirror. "Well, ugly as it is, I'm proud of it." Then the nightmare came. Now there are only questions with no simple answers.

—*Sports Illustrated, November 22, 1982*

BITTERSWEET TWILIGHT
FOR SUGAR RAY

When thirty-one-year-old Sugar Ray Leonard agreed to fight middleweight champion Marvin Hagler in 1987, many wondered why the former champ would come out of retirement to face certain defeat. Once again, Leonard defied his critics and won the bout. To understand why some fighters keep going, Wiley paid a visit to the original Sugar Ray, Ray Robinson, for this Sports Illustrated *profile.*

"To be a great champion, you must believe you are the best. If you're not, pretend you are."—MUHAMMAD ALI**

In the fall of 1986, Sugar Ray Leonard signed to fight Marvelous Marvin Hagler. Soon after, a question arose about Leonard. People are civilized now, for the most part, and asked, "Why is he doing it?" Not "Can he win?" but "Why would he risk it?" Was it the money, a guaranteed $11 million? Was it an irrepressible urge that goes with having been a champion? Was it merely ego, a grab for a higher place in boxing history?

No one thought to ask the uncivilized people. Men have lived warmed by the fire of civilization for so long that they have forgotten what it takes to survive with nothing but their wits and bare hands to fend off the jackals that stalk them. So the men who had forgotten this, or had convinced themselves they had, continued to ask, "Why?"

I went to see a man who knows why. He wasn't too hard to find.

"Ray."

No answer.

"Ray."

"Nnnnn."

"Ray."

"Nnn?"

"Can Sugar Ray Leonard beat Marvelous Marvin Hagler?"

Sugar Ray Robinson didn't answer. It might have been that he couldn't answer. That would seem most likely. There is the advancing Alzheimer's disease to consider and the medication he is regularly given. He also has diabetes and hypertension. Beyond all this, there are the terrible lessons that 201 fights over twenty-five years have etched on his mind. Finally, there is Millie, his wife of twenty-two years. Any or all of these could be reasons why Robinson didn't answer. But it also could have been that he chose not to answer. The one incontrovertible truth is that Sugar Ray Robinson earned his silence the hard way. He didn't have to say anything. He left all the answers in the ring.

The sixty-five-year-old former nonpareil welterweight and five-time middleweight champion smiled, then looked toward his lap. He was watched by Millie Robinson, who sat nearby in the modest offices of the Sugar Ray Robinson Youth Foundation, on Crenshaw Boulevard in the mid-Wilshire section of Los Angeles. It was November 1986. The board of directors of the foundation was meeting. Ray sat at the head of the table, his paper plate laden with meat and exotic fruit. He had not taken a bite. He had no appetite. Business was discussed by six other board members, the officers of his legacy. Robinson was oblivious. He was in his own world.

"Ray will still talk, sometimes, a little bit," Sid Lockitch had said earlier at his office in Century City. Lockitch, an accountant, has been Robinson's business manager for more than 20 years and is the treasurer of the foundation. "When Millie's not around, he'll say a word or two. But even years ago, Ray was always a gentleman. He would never have said that Marvin Hagler is going to beat the crap out of Sugar Ray Leonard. He would have said luck to them both."

The telephone rang at the foundation office. For Millie.

"Ray, can Leonard beat Hagler?"

Robinson's smile became even broader, even more vacant. Then he leaned close. "Is he sweeter than me?" he asked, cloaking that once satiny voice in a whisper. I conspired with him.

"No, Ray."

In the spring of 1987, on Monday, April 6, Ray Leonard (33-1), the former welterweight and junior middleweight champion, fought middleweight champion Marvelous Marvin Hagler (62-2-2) in Las Vegas. Leonard, thirty-one, came into the ring after a layoff of more than 1,000 days and with a surgically repaired left eye. The question still hung in the air. Why? Leonard was already known as the greatest welterweight since Robinson. Leonard could never be considered greater than Robinson. Not unless he fought, say, a hundred more times. Certainly not unless he somehow beat Hagler. "I care nothing for history," Leonard said on the Friday before the fight. So saying, he did the improbable—he beat the bigger, stronger man, just as Muhammad Ali had done, more impressively, against Sonny Liston and George Foreman.

"Ali absolutely worshiped Ray," Sid Lockitch says. "Still does. Usually, the greatest fall from grace is by fighters. People tend to avoid ex-fighters. They feel they took one too many. Randy Turpin once asked Ray, 'What's worse, being a has-been or a never-was?' Then Randy committed suicide. But the people never forgot Ray. He felt God had made him a boxer for that reason. So he would not be forgotten. So he could help."

It is eerie, the similarity in technique between the three of them—first Robinson, then Ali, now Leonard. It was Robinson who was the original, the handsome master boxer with matchless hand speed, charisma, and the fine legs of a figure skater. It was Robinson who went 123-1-2 to begin his career and become the welterweight champion, and it was Robinson who then went on to win the middleweight title those incredible five times. Yet, it was also Robinson who lost six times while fighting for the middleweight title. He won the national Golden Gloves featherweight title in 1939 at age seventeen, when Joe Louis was heavyweight champion of the world. He lost his final fight at forty-four, to the No. 1 middleweight contender, Joey Archer, in 1965, when Ali was champ. In the years from 1945 to the middle of 1951, Robinson, at 147 pounds, was unbeatable and irresistible. To the men of that era, and to some of their many sons and daughters, Leonard can only be a Sugar substitute.

"I like Ray Leonard," says Irving Rudd, sixty-nine, a veteran boxing publicist with Bob Arum's Top Rank, Inc., promoters of the Leonard-Hagler fight. "I think a lot of him as a fighter. That's why I say that, at his very fittest, he might have gone five rounds before Ray Robinson knocked him out. Five rounds, I say. Tops."

"He was the greatest. A distance fighter. A half-distance fighter. An in-fighter. Scientific. He was wonderful to see." Max Schmeling once said that of Robinson.

"The greatest fighter ever to step into the ring." Joe Louis once said that.

"The greatest . . . pound-for-pound," wrote the late columnist Jimmy Cannon, who, it is said, was impressed by hardly anyone— except Sugar Ray. When Ali was champ, the acerbic Cannon told him to enjoy it while he could, because the jackals would come for him one day.

In February 1964, when he was still known as Cassius Clay, a long shot who was about to fight Liston for the heavyweight title, Ali had invoked the name of Robinson, who was in Miami for the bout. "You tell Sonny Liston I'm here with Sugar Ray!" In a weigh-in performance that almost assuredly convinced Liston that he would be defending his title against a madman, Ali screamed to the press at the top of his lungs. "Sugar Ray and I are two pretty dancers. We can't be beat."

"Ray was the pro's pro," says Rudd. "When they told him he had a fight, Ray never asked who the opponent was or where the fight was going to be. Ray only asked, 'How much?'"

The general reaction of the middle-aged and older American public to Sugar Ray Robinson could best be summed up by a reminiscence of the late Red Smith. Smith was reminded of Robinson while visiting the zoo one day. When the columnist stood transfixed at the cage where a jaguar paced back and forth, he gazed at the superbly muscled predator and said, "Good morning, Ray. You're looking good, Ray."

Ray isn't looking so good anymore. "It's very painful to see him like this. The situation is not going to get any better," Lockitch says. Lockitch is referring to Robinson's deteriorating health, but another officer of the youth foundation adds, "It's like Ray is in prison. Millie treats him like a child. She lets him go nowhere with no one. Not even his own son."

Robinson's thirty-seven-year-old son, Ray Jr., says, "My father is virtually being held captive."

I had only wanted to go with Sugar Ray to the barbershop and ask him if Leonard could beat Hagler, and how. That's all. I knew Robinson still went to the barbershop at least once a week, sometimes more often. So I asked Millie about it and she said, "I take care of Uncle Wright. He's eighty-seven. I take care of Ray. He's my husband. I love him. I've been what I've been to him for all these years. I could hire help, but I don't mind doing it. I don't need help. I have tears in my eyes, I'm trying so hard. Ray's going to get better. He's not better now. He's not going to the barbershop with you because I'm by his side every minute. He goes to five different barbershops. Only I know which ones. My husband is not a yo-yo for people to jerk around as they please. I'm in charge now. I take care of Ray. I'm the one in control."

"Now . . . ." Millie fixes me with a defiant gaze. There's only one thing she wants to know. She asks, "How much?"

It might seem odd, wanting to watch Sugar Ray Robinson get his hair cut. But, being one of the younger baby-boomers, I am not old enough to remember what it was like to see the Sugar fight in his prime, much less to anticipate his fights, to go through the sweet agony of not knowing . . . and then to be so utterly convinced by his skill. I had missed the pleasure of that tension. I had only seen the old films. The fights had long been decided, the participants' places in history secured.

I first learned of the emotion stirred by Sugar Ray when, as a boy, I went to the barbershop, that sanctuary of masculinity and tonic with the striped pole outside. Inside, hair fell to the floor and the smell of talc hung in the air. Cokes cost a dime. Razor straps were used for their intended purpose. It was a place that buzzed. Great lies and great truths were tossed about like glances.

When I was a boy in the barbershop, one name would come up louder than the rest. The name was Cassius Clay. There would be a great deal of murmuring assent—and an occasional derisive sneer—that a real tough guy would eventually show the kid what for. Probably Liston. Then someone would reply: "Liston won't see what hit him. And neither will you." But there was at least one barber—he almost always seemed to be the one holding a pair of scissors perilously close to my ear—who would become agitated and say, "Hold on. Let's get it straight in here. That boy is good. He's good. But he ain't no Ray Robinson. There ain't but one Sugar—and Sugar give you diabetes quick."

After Ali had gone through the best part of his career and had endured a three-year layoff because of his refusal to be drafted, he signed to fight Oscar Bonavena on Dec. 7, 1970. That was to be a warmup before his real comeback fight—his epic loss to Joe Frazier in Madison Square Garden in March 1971. At the weigh-in with Bonavena, the Argentine attempted to get Ali's goat. He succeeded, to his later sorrow. "Clay? Clay?" Bonavena mocked. He spoke little English. "Clay . . . Why you no go in ahrrmy? You cheeken? Peep-peep-peep . . . peep-peep-peep."

A look came over Ali's face that I had not seen before—true anger. Usually, Ali was like Robinson, and Ray usually held his temper. "Don't get mad," Robinson liked to say. "Get even."

Ali grimly asked Bonavena what seemed to be a curious question: "Did you cut your hair?"

"Whaat?" replied Bonavena.

"Did you cut your hair?"

"Whaat?"

"I'll cut your hair," said a deadpan Ali, who would knock out Bonavena in the fifteenth round.

Robinson, for his part, had a nickname for his youngest son.

From the time Ray Jr. was a child his father has called him "Trimmer."

"Oh sure, Ray loves to get his hair cut. Loves it," Lockitch says. "He's still vain that way. He wouldn't dream of going anywhere without going to the barbershop. Whenever he'd go to New York, that was the first thing he'd do."

Before he became the fighter's business manager, before he became involved with the foundation, Lockitch was one of the men for whom Robinson was the Sugar. Lockitch became Ray's friend when Ray and Millie moved to Los Angeles, back in '65, right after they were married in Vegas. Lockitch was there when the foundation idea was first proposed in 1969, in Millie Robinson's kitchen in the lime green duplex on the corner of West Adams Boulevard and 10th Avenue. The house is owned by 87-year-old Wright Fillmore.

Millie and Ray still live on the second floor; "Uncle" Wright lives on the first. Fillmore, who was a close friend of Millie's parents, is president of the foundation and has been a benefactor of Ray's since 1965. Over the years, he has been the owner of a lot of property on West Adams.

"Ray used to say he knew every man," says Lockitch. "Ask him if he knew the chairman of the board for Standard Oil and Ray would say, 'Sure.' What Ray meant was that the guy knew him. All he had to do was call and say 'This is Sugar Ray Robinson,' and the guy would know who he was and do whatever he could to help Ray out."

Ray Robinson's world was a man's world. Women were differ-ent, except for his mother, Leila Smith. Women were to be won. They were part of the spoils of war. Even Ray's mother could not completely displace Ray from his male constituency. After young Walker Smith, fighting under the assumed named of Ray Robinson, emerged from anonymity in 1939—by boxing like a dream and being nicknamed Sugar because he fought so sweet-ly—he was visited by his father, Walker Smith Sr., whom the newly minted Sugar Ray Robinson had not seen in eight years. Robinson happily shelled out some bucks to his pop. When Ray later told his mother what had happened, she was indignant. Walker Smith had walked out on her. On them. Said Robinson to his mother, "That's your business."

Still, she was his mother and his biggest fan. "It didn't matter what weight they were. He was the best, says Leila Smith. It's a cold day in January 1987, and she is sitting in apartment she shares her daughter, Evelyn Nelson, on University Avenue in the South Bronx. For a woman of eighty-nine years, Leila Smith is full of wit and vitality. Her memory is sharp.

"That [Joey] Maxim fight. That's the one that Ray shouldn't have had," she says. "The only one."

During his career, Robinson had twenty or more bouts like the one Leonard undertook with Hagler. After overwhelming the wel-terweights of his day, Robinson moved up to middleweight in 1950 and was involved in stirring battles with the likes of Jake LaMotta, Randy Turpin, Carmen Basilio, Gene Fullmer, Bobo

Olson, and Paul Pender. He was not the same fighter at the heavier weight, 160 pounds. He was still a great fighter, but he was not the unbeatable Sugar. Then, on June 25, 1952, when he was thirty-one, Robinson climbed into a ring that had been set up in Yankee Stadium to fight Joey Maxim for the light heavyweight title.

"It was 104 degrees that night. It was 130 degrees ringside, that's what they said. I was there. It felt like it," says Leila Smith. "Whatever you call 'great' nowadays, I guess Ray was that then. I went to his fights. I wasn't superstitious. When Ray sat between rounds that night, I dropped my head. People said, 'Why do you drop your head? You crying?' I was praying."

Robinson wore black that night. His mother wore white. Ray had already won the middleweight title from LaMotta, lost it to Turpin, then regained it from Turpin; then he defended it by decisioning Olson and again by knocking out Rocky Graziano with one perfect right in the third round in Chicago. The right was so devastating that Graziano lay stretched out on the canvas with his right leg twitching.

The whole world seemed to be Sugar Ray's oyster, and the Maxim fight would showcase him in his backyard. Robinson was the pride of Harlem, but admiration of his abilities was not restricted to people of his race. Black heavyweight champions like Jack Johnson and Louis had to bear heavy sociological burdens whether they liked it or not. Ray straightened his hair and he was the Sugar to everybody. "Color means nothing to him," Lockitch says.

It seemed that Ray had many friends when he stepped into the ring to fight Maxim in the sweltering early summer heat and under a battery of hot lights. "I had won welter and middle, beaten most of the people in my class," Ray said once. "People wanted to see me fight Maxim."

Maxim's given name was Giuseppe Antonio Berardinelli. He was born in Cleveland. He was strong even for a six-foot-one, 175-pounder, and he was an earnest campaigner. He had fought 99 times before he met Robinson. He had won seventy-eight times, drawn four. He had been knocked out only once and was better than any light heavyweight in the world except Ezzard Charles, to whom he had lost five times, and Jersey Joe Walcott, who had beaten him twice. As a boxer, Maxim was not in Robinson's class, but he was still an excellent fighter—and two classes above Ray in natural weight. Maxim was thirty years old and the light-heavy champ almost by default, since Charles and Walcott had moved up to heavyweight to meet their fates at the hands of each other and Rocky Marciano. Maxim himself had fought once for the heavyweight title, losing to Charles in 1951.

At the end of the tenth round, the referee, on the verge of collapse, had to quit and a substitute took over. "The world swam before my eyes," says Leila Smith. And it swam before Robinson's. He had used his brilliant moves and blinding hand speed to hit Maxim with every punch in his repertoire. In the seventh, he nailed Maxim with the perfect right—similar to the one that had left Graziano twitching. Maxim was turned sideways by the force of the punch but he did not go down. The light-heavy was too big. Robinson couldn't hurt him. At the end of the thirteenth, Robinson, well ahead on all cards, was done in by the heat. He staggered across the ring into the arms of his cornermen. He could not answer the bell for the fourteenth round. If the fight had gone twelve rounds, he would have won. Robinson announced his retirement that December.

"Ray had promised me back in 1940 that I would never have to work again," says Leila Smith. "And I never had to. My son always took care of me."

Upon retirement, Robinson set out for Europe, ostensibly to begin a second career as a tap-dancing troubador and to enjoy the spoils of war. He had been married on May 29, 1944, to Edna-Mae Holly, a beautiful show girl who, in 1949, had borne him Jr. Edna Mae would later have four miscarriages. Robinson was a man of extravagant tastes, appetites, and generosity. He could eat a dozen doughnuts and wash them down with a pitcher of sweet tea. He ordered fuchsia Cadillacs, first-class staterooms, and the finest of champagnes for his valets, golf pros, chauffeurs, secretaries, and, of course, his barbers. "He wanted to buy me a Cadillac," says Leila Smith. "But I only saw hard men and rough women in those cars. So he bought me a Buick."

Robinson was back in the ring within two years. "Sure, I could use a buck as well as the next guy," he said. "But this was not the reason. I just had the feeling. I got the urge. People wanted to see me fight."

Robinson's ring career would continue for another eleven years and twice more he would hold the middleweight title, but he was never again a god. In 1960, he separated from Edna-Mae, and in the twilight of his boxing days he married Millie Bruce and moved to L.A.

"Now, for four or five years, I don't get nothing, I don't hear nothing," says Leila Smith. "And I don't ask why. Ray had been sick only one day in his life. Pneumonia. Maybe food poisoning. It was before a fight. I had to go to Philadelphia because he would-n't go to the hospital. He called the hospital a good place to die. He didn't ride elevators, either. Ray is not a man to be trapped."

Five years ago, Robinson fell ill but wouldn't allow Millie to hos-pitalize him. So Millie sent for Leila Smith. Millie had suffered at Ray's hand physically and she had temporarily moved out. Frank Sinatra, an old friend, called Robinson and told him that Millie would come back to the house if Ray agreed to be hospitalized. But it took Ray's mother to finally convince him to put himself in the doctor's hands.

"The doctor who examined him at the house said his blood sugar was very high. So I went out there," recalls Mrs. Smith. "He wouldn't go to the hospital for nobody but me. He seemed to be delirious. He got upset whenever she [Millie] came near. It was her. Just her. I could go and talk to him. But her—she had gone away, and Ray was waiting for her on the porch. She said Ray had knocked her down before. I told her, 'You better do something or Ray will hurt you.' Sugar is dangerous, you know.

She didn't seem to know what was wrong with him.

"That was the last time I saw him. I used to talk to him on the phone. Sometimes, he would repeat himself. Sometimes he'd say, 'Ma, I didn't mean it.'"

Leila Smith took "it" to mean Jimmy Doyle. On June 23, 1947, the night before Robinson fought Doyle in Cleveland, Ray dreamed he killed Doyle with a single left hook. The next morning, a shaken Sugar told his manager, George Gainford, and the fight promoters that he couldn't go into the ring against Doyle, but the promoters brought in a Catholic priest who assured Robinson his fears were unfounded. The fight must go on, that night. In the eighth round, Sugar hit Doyle with a textbook left hook. Doyle was taken out of the ring on a stretcher. He died the next day without ever regaining consciousness.

"He meant Doyle. I know my son. But . . . I can't be sure," says Leila Smith. "Ray used to take care of me. I used to know him. To me, Millie is a Johnny-come-lately. I don't know much about this last marriage."

Mildred Bruce, several years Ray's senior, had two sons and a daughter by a previous marriage. Her younger son died at an early age. The other son, Herman, fifty, is now called Butch Robinson. He helps run the activities program for the foundation. "She got her son named Robinson," says Leila Smith. "But when little Ray [Ray Jr.] went out there, he was pushed to the back. Just like Leonard. Just took Ray's glory. Millie doesn't care who doesn't like what. She keeps Ray shut away because somebody would see how bad off he is. Evelyn says it's bad. My chances of ever seeing Ray again are poor. If I didn't have Jesus, I wouldn't survive. I would lose my mind. It would hurt me not to be able to even talk to Ray. It brings tears to my eyes just to think about him. I want to do what's right, but what is right these days?"

Later, I talk to Millie. She is upset, which is not good because she suffers from hypertension. "So, you went and talked to Ray's mother behind my back," she says.

"No, Mrs. Robinson. Not behind your back. Mrs. Smith is Ray's mother. She was very kind."

"Well, I'm his wife."

Leila Smith mentioned when I visited that she was a little bit tired. On Monday morning, Feb. 9, 1987, just after midnight, she suffered gastric distress. She was quickly hospitalized and underwent emergency surgery for an intestinal blockage. She was not strong enough to survive the trauma. Before morning light, the mother of the greatest boxer pound-for-pound that ever lived, died in a small room at Montefiore Medical Center in the Bronx.

"Ray."

"Nnn?"

"Do you miss New York?"

". . . Well, sure."

A chill wind whips over the burial grounds of Ferncliff Cemetery in Hartsdale, New York, causing the small gathering of mourners to huddle closer together and pull their winter coats tight. It is Valentine's Day. Edna-Mae Robinson holds her hand over her mouth and leans toward her son, Ray Jr., as the minister says simple words over the casket bearing the remains of Leila Smith.

A large wreath of white carnations stands at the head of the open grave. The banner bears the script: YOUR SON, SUGAR RAY. Blood-red boxing gloves are pinned to the center of the arrangement. Once the minister has finished and the mourners have moved reluctantly away, the gloves are removed by the boldest of the male relatives. Some carnations are plucked as melancholy souvenirs. A letter from Ray to his mother was read at the funeral service. Ray was not present. Millie has to help him when he goes to the bathroom, so a transcontinental trip seemed out of the question.

"Oh, I'm real clear on what kind of person Millie is," says Ray Jr. "I guess she doesn't want him in these surroundings any-more. Or out from under the influence of medication. My father is virtually in prison, yes, but it's a strange kind of prison. He can be pumped up to go to a party at Frank Sinatra's house, but he can't come to his own mother's funeral." Actually, Ray Robinson had been hospitalized the day before his mother's funeral. He had become agitated and his blood sugar had risen.

Seven years ago, Ray Jr. moved to Venice, California, to work for the foundation and spend some time with his father. He never got that time—and he never got the job. "My dad had written me an amazing letter. I was thrilled at the chance to get to know him. My father had always been a . . . businessman. His business kept him away. But he wrote and said he wanted me to work with him. When I got there, I was shocked. He weighed 215 pounds. For six-and-a-half years, I've lived not twenty minutes from them. I been in their house no more than ten times—most times uninvited."

"I don't want any problems with Millie," says Edna-Mae. "I don't want anything. I used to be the first lady. But she is now. When I found out Ray was sick, I sent out literature on high blood pressure and diabetes and Alzheimer's, and she became very upset. Why? My son was in for a rude awakening when he went out there."

Sugar Ray remained fit for ten years after he retired in '65. He worked out nearly every day, either on the road or with the bags. Lockitch tried to introduce him to health clubs, but Robinson went into one, looked around, and said, "This ain't a gym. It's got to look like a gym. It's got to smell like a gym." And so he went off to find a real gym, and he continued working out until 1975, when he finally let it go. But he couldn't really let it go. After all, he was still the Sugar. That would never change.

"It hurt me when they started calling this new young man Sugar Ray," says Edna-Mae. "It must have hurt Ray." If it did, he didn't show it. Robinson posed for a few photographs with Leonard and never said an unkind word about his fistic namesake and heir.

For a time, Robinson was fanatical about the Dodgers. He became a friend of manager Tommy Lasorda. All it took was an introduction. One day at Dodger Stadium when Sylvester Stallone, the cinematic heavyweight champion, was there, a fan asked to shake the actor's hand. Stallone's bodyguard said, "Mr. Stallone doesn't like to be touched." Then Stallone spotted Sugar Ray. His bodyguard asked Robinson if they could meet. Ray sent a message over. "Mr. Robinson doesn't like to be touched." Ray had enjoyed that.

But baseball and one-upmanship could not satisfy Robinson's soul. Robinson remained a womanizer until the diabetes, hypertension, and Alzheimer's began to take their toll. Millie was no fool. Neither was Edna-Mae. When Gainford died in 1981, Ray made a trip to New York unaccompanied by Millie, but with a bodyguard. After the funeral service, Ray met Edna-Mae and suggested they go to his hotel together. "I told him I couldn't do that; we weren't married anymore," says Edna-Mae. "He got very upset. I had to tell his bodyguard to please take him away, because I didn't want to get hurt." Robinson returned to California and Millie.

"I could never understand Millie's attitude," says Edna-Mae. "At first I thought it was just because she was afraid she might not get power of attorney. But she has that. She's his wife. But Ray is his son. Leila was his mother. They should have been allowed in his life. That letter they read at the funeral—Ray didn't write that. It was signed, but he didn't sign it, either. In my seventeen years with him, when I think of all the thousands of pictures that I signed, 'Good luck, Sugar Ray' . . . so I know. That letter wasn't from him. I don't know what Millie is doing. I suppose she's trying to keep alive the myth of Ray's competence."

"Ray."

"Nnnn."

Katy Riney is the program administrator of the Sugar Ray Robinson Youth Foundation. It was Riney who drafted the letter and sent the floral arrangement to Leila Smith's funeral. These were merely two of her many duties as the foundation's most indispensable employee. And if the foundation were Robinson's only legacy, it would be a good legacy, the very best. Since the organization became active in 1969, thousands of inner-city children have had constructive activities to fill their idle weekends—from volleyball and flag football to pageants and talent shows. The foundation sponsors no boxing programs.

On one Saturday morning, 100 girls are playing volleyball in the gymnasium at Bethune Junior High in South-Central Los Angeles. It is some weeks before the Leonard-Hagler fight. Riney referees and takes the girls through their paces, team by team. Outside, 150 boys under the supervision of Butch Robinson play flag football. There are six community directors present at Bethune. Most have been with the foundation for ten years or more. One of them is forty-year-old Reniell Beard.

"I've got all Ray's fights on tape," says Beard. "I had four older brothers. Ray was like a god to them. They stopped me from watching *The Amos and Andy Show* and made me watch Sugar Ray's fights. I guess that's why I do this. It's like repaying a debt. It's nice to do something for the kids, although most of them have no idea who Sugar Ray Robinson is."

One look at these kids at play, keeping amused and interested amid some of the most depressing urban blight to be found in America—in South-Central Los Angeles some apartment houses have their street numbers painted on the roofs, the better for police helicopter pilots to identify the buildings—is enough to create genuine admiration for this tangible part of Robinson's legacy.

Michael Dear, thirteen, has been involved with various foundation programs for one year. I ask him if he knows about Sugar Ray Robinson. "Yeah," he says. "He's fightin' in April." No, that's Sugar Ray Leonard. Sugar Ray Robinson.

"They are not the same?"

Jattea Johnson, sixteen, has been in the program for four years and is now in high school. She still comes by on weekends. It is a good habit she doesn't want to break. "I know Sugar Ray Robinson is an ex-boxer," she says. "All I know is that one Sugar Ray is older than the other one."

"That's O.K.," says Beard. "And as far as the fight goes, the referee will call it before nine. Leonard is in there with a warmonger."

The Sugar Ray Robinson Youth Foundation must pass the scrutiny of the California state legislature every year, and satisfy the state auditors. It won its funding in the first place because former governor Edmund "Pat" Brown was a great fan of Robinson's. "Dollar for dollar, we're the best bargain they have," Lockitch says.

The foundation receives approximately $488,000 a year from the state and $50,000 from Los Angeles County, and this year it got $71,000 from the Olympic Games surplus funds. Some of the money goes for the buses that transport the children to the activities and pageants. Robinson, as the titular head of the foundation, receives a salary of $37,000. "Millie needs that stipend," says Riney.

And so that is why Millie asked, "How much?" Not that she is to be blamed—no more than Robinson was to be blamed for being paid to fight. You use what you have. Butch received money from a gossip tabloid for "revealing" that Ray had Alzheimer's. Evelyn Nelson's son, Kenneth, asked Millie for permission to use Sugar Ray's name for an Urban Coalition fundraiser, in conjunction with a showing of the Leonard-Hagler fight at the Apollo Theater in Harlem. (Millie said yes, then at the last minute changed her mind and informed the Urban Coalition that she was withdrawing her permission. It was decided that the event would have to be canceled.)

When Robinson became ill after his mother's death, he was admitted to the Cedars-Sinai Medical Center in Los Angeles. He remained hospitalized for a week. A few days after he was released, Robinson sat in their yellow Cadillac while Millie went into the foundation offices. Ray no longer wore the vacant smile. I came over and spoke to him. "Ray. How can Ray beat Marvin Hagler?" He didn't respond.

"I don't expect the fight to last long," Ray Jr. had said when he was asked for a prediction. "My father did it, but he always had tune-up fights. And he's my father. There was no one else like him. He was Sugar Ray."

But Leonard did win. He defeated Hagler, in 12 rounds. He is the Sugar now.

Leonard is not to be asked why he fought Hagler. "Why?" is a nervy question to ask a prizefighter. As Robinson often said, "Because it's what people want to see." Leonard fights for us as much as he fights for himself. Like Robinson, like a lot of other people, he can't separate who he is from what he does best.

Sugar Ray Robinson is no different from Sugar Ray Leonard. What he did best was fight. Like Leonard, he's not to be asked why he fought, and these days he can't be asked much of anything. He did indeed leave all the answers in the ring. But Ray Jr. had one thing exactly right about him. While his father may no longer be the Sugar, there was—and is—no one else like him.

—*Sports Illustrated, July 13, 1987*

TOO LATE TO
SAVE TYSON

2002, Mike Tyson's boxing career was far from the one Wiley had envisioned for him sixteen years earlier. With Tyson's reputation in the ring now a disgrace, Wiley, in this ESPN.com column, finally says, "No mas."

Someone I like enormously was at the press conference the other day when Little Mike Tyson went off. I say Little, because when Tyson came down off his little pedestal and sauntered over to Lennox Lewis, it occurred to me—the only way Tyson could beat Lewis about the head and shoulders was with a tennis racket.

And then only by using an overhand smash technique.

Lewis may be mild-mannered, but he ain't no short lob to be put away. He requires work. Maybe this occurred to Tyson, too. Maybe he was feeling like he wanted to stand nose-to-nose with Lennox Lewis, and then discovered he could only stand nose-to-sternum.

So he destroyed the photo op.

So throw a Napoleonic complex in on top of all the other horrors and schizophrenia involved with being Tyson. You've got insanity. Which fits. In a way: Boxing is insane, schizophrenic. Something sociopathic about it. In short, something like . . . well, let's hope not like you and me. But we can find out if it is. The rest of this piece will also be schizophrenic, the better to reflect its subject matter.

First, let's clean up the rest of the Tyson mess, coming as it does in the Glacial Wait for the Lewis-Tyson heavyweight title fight.

I relied on experts and history for my background on this matter, and my jacket on Tyson. First, Maxie K. Maxie is a very young man whom we admire for his passion for the bloodsport. He thinks Mike Tyson might be trying to get out of the fight, and that Fear is a major element in his latest meltdown—fear and abject desperation. He may have a point, but I myself would fight Lucifer for half of what Tyson stands to gain against Lewis. Then again, Tyson ain't broke. But if he's feeding all his hangers-on, he soon may be.

Who *are* these people? The ones always surrounding Tyson? It looks like the Boys Choir of Harlem, so tightly are they packed in like sardines on top of one another—only these ain't nobody's boys.

Does Bed-Stuy close whenever Tyson goes to a press conference?

It's sad; really, pathetic. He can no more rid himself of them than a shark can rid itself of more fish and the constant need for motion.

Ali was much bigger, and Ali's entourage wasn't a third this size. And in fact, all the people around Ali had a purpose in furthering his fighting abilities: Luis Sarria, the silent Cuban masseuse; Dr. Ferdie Pacheco, the Weeping Medic; Angelo, always Angelo; Pat Patterson, the Chicago cop bodyguard. Really, Ali had only one hanger-on, Bundini Brown, who was paid to be an a–hole. The rest of them had a purpose. No one around Tyson has any purpose at all. His corner is a joke and always has been. It's hard to go down from Kevin Rooney, but Tyson has sunk far beneath that.

I saw it all a few years ago, when I saw Tyson at his digs in Vegas. He had invited me over. Why, I don't know. I have been known to write about fighters, probably that's why. In order to get into the inner sanctum, where he was sitting all alone, I had to pass through a phalanx of maybe twenty dudes—dudes who were about nothing, dudes who were into nothing, dudes who had nothing to offer. They were the essence of street bravado, their skills were only in offering and cheering lame insults, and their only concern was where their next meal, or lay, or gaudy piece of outerwear was coming from. If I sound hard on them, well, they passed themselves off as hard men; they probably would kill you if there was a couple grand or some perceived disrespect involved in it, if they had a chance and thought they could escape punishment—they certainly looked as if they wanted to kill me, or at least beat me, for coming and gaining private access to the meal ticket.

Suppose I took him away from them? Suppose I told him he didn't need them, there was another way—the Way of the Intercepting Fist? Suppose we rented Bruce Lee movies and kicked it a while?

But more likely, these hangers-on would simple drag Tyson down further into the muck of the netherworld, and they did, and he is stuck there now, seemingly for good. So this is nothing new in boxing or life. In the streets, attrition rates have always been high.

Emanuel escaped. I recall when Emanuel Steward took me into his home in Detroit, where his lovely wife prepared a delicious dinner that was also low in fat. With the death of Gentleman Eddie Futch, Steward became the best trainer in boxing, guided the remorseless, prolific, bed-hopping Evander Holyfield to the title, then guided the massive, polite, proper, almost prim but well-coordinated Lewis to same. And let's not forget his work with once underfed Thomas Hearns, and a cadre of other boys-beyond-boyhood who made a buck or two, coming out of that hellhole, the Kronk Gym.

But Emanuel once was just a cheap little bully himself, when he was kid, cruising the streets for battle scars. He found the hidden discipline that lies at the bottom of boxing and improved himself. But he'll tell you today that as a boy, he was nothing but a hellion.

George Foreman may be no great shakes as a boxing broadcaster, but he cooks one hell of a hamburger. People boast of having this George Foreman grill, that renders the fat away from meat in a clean fashion, almost as well as Mrs. Steward did, and much the way George used to stoically knock dudes out—no muss, no fuss.

George had terrorized the streets of the brutal Third Ward in Houston for years before he became a professional boxer. He was a bully. He waved the flag at the '68 Olympics when he won heavy gold; patriotism is the easiest way to foment an uneasy tolerance of oneself, if one needs to foment that. Especially when other black dudes are standing on medal stands wearing black gloves. Still, George was never seen as being more than two steps away from becoming Sonny Liston, or some other sociopathic bully boxer.

After George was beaten by Ali in Zaire, he signed to fight a platoon of heavyweights, all on one night in New York. He fought five, six, seven men on that strange evening. I remember thinking, "George, no matter how many of them you knock out, this is what you have to figure out—it's *you* that you have to beat."

Somebody's probably been talking that Sun-Tzu-Art-of-War smack to Tyson, as well. Apparently, he ain't hearing it as well.

So my circle of wisdom was complete. Maxie K., through the life and times of Emanuel Steward, through the miraculously changed public face of George Foreman, ending with, who else, Road Dog.

"Didya hear about Tyson?" said Dog. He sounded so very sad, I didn't even taunt him about both of them being from Brooklyn.

"It's pretty bad," I said. "It's a weirdly nobly barbaric event, a boxing title fight. I've known few who could make it—or the run-up to it—seem otherwise. It's a dark thing. That was the genius of Ali. He made it seem like such a lark. I've seen three men die in the ring, beaten to death right before my eyes. I suppose it requires a greater discipline for the participants to say, 'We who are about to die salute you.' Apparently, Tyson's not in the mood for that."

"What can he do now?" asked Dog.

"Fight. That's about it. What can any of us do?" I replied. "So, do you want to set up a meeting. In Brooklyn? On Tyson's territory? Where you'll be safe? Easy enough to do. Just hail any nefarious-looking, corner-hanging dude on the street in Brooklyn. He's probably a Tyson hanger-on. Want to try and rehabilitate him, Dog? I think, if you want to do that, that you'll be fighting all day. But it *would* keep you alert. Do you want to get to the bottom of the screaming wail that is the mind of Mike Tyson, do you really want to touch the maggots that are chewing away at his soul . . . . ?

". . . . the ship . . . be sunk," said Dog, sadly.

Stunned. Never heard of Dog throwing in the towel. He still thinks the Dodgers are coming back and is saving money to contribute to a new stadium. He thinks the Knicks are one player away. But he's given up on Tyson. What power the Ex-Heavyweight Champion still has! What emotions he does fire! How in hell does he do it?

Take this test and see. Call it the Mike Tyson Pop Psych Profile. Dog took it, and now he feels better. Got exactly one laugh out of it. Scoring done by three judges, not including Dr. Flip Homansky.

What would have been Ali's nickname for Tyson, had they fought?

a. Yum-Yum Eat Em Up

b. Brainiac

c. Red Skull

d. Where Is He? Oh, Down There

Who would be the best trainer for Tyson?

a. Slobodan Milosevic

b. Siegfreid & Roy

c. Shane Mosley's dad

d. Emanuel Steward; difficult though, because Steward is also Lewis's trainer; maybe he'd alternate corners by round. If both boxers get in trouble, he could whip out the cellie and consult.

What is the best music for Tyson to box by?

a. "Loving You"

b. "It's The End Of The World As We Know It"

c. The gangster rap of Biggie Smalls

d. Schzoid screaming guitars and bats blowing saxophones

Who was older, Tyson now, or Ali in the Rumble in the Jungle?

a. Who cares?

b. Tyson was born of woman?

c. Ali

d. Tyson

Who should write a book about Tyson?

a. Pete Vecsey

b. Martha Stewart

c. Bret Easton Ellis

d. Clive Barker

Who should direct the inevitable movie about Tyson?

a. Wolfgang Puck

b. John Carpenter

c. Spike Lee

d. Martin Scorsese

Who should play Tyson in said movie?

a. Denzel Washington

b. Jaime Foxx

c. Michael Clarke Duncan

d. Whoever he is, I don't want to meet him

Who Is Tyson's favorite writer?

a. Pete Vecsey

b. Jose Torres

c. Print Is Dead

d. Harlan Ellison, author of *I Have No Mouth & I Must Scream*

What would Howard Cosell say about Tyson?

a. "Down goes Lewis!" Down goes Lewis!" Then he'd wake up.

b. "Comparatively, Frank Gifford is a intellectual lightweight."

c. "I will broadcast no more forever . . . ."

d. "Oh, the tawdriness, the mindlessness, the residuals . . . ."

Should boxing be banned?

a. No

b. *Hell* no!

c. Yes

d. Boxing could never be banned, so why are discussing it?

Why are we even discussing boxing?

a. Slow day at the water cooler

b. Because nothing else can challenge the Rams

c. Shane Mosley, Roy Jones Jr., a raft of lesser champions

d. Mike Tyson

Can Mike Tyson beat Lennox Lewis?

a. It depends on the height of the stepladder

b. It depends on who brings up the word "gay" first

c. Beat him at what? Insulting sportswriters?

d. Any man with two hands in the ring is dangerous. Even an insane one. Maybe *especially* an insane one.

Which way would you bet?

a. Lewis

b. Tyson

c. Even money the fight doesn't come off at all

d. I wouldn't

Give yourself 5 points for every (a) answer; 4 points for every (b) answer; 2 points for every (c) answer; 1 point for every (d) answer.

If you didn't take this test at all, award yourself 0 points. 50-65 points: Why, you're a bigger sociopath than Tyson. 35-50 points: You're more of a Bundini Brown sociopath. 20-35 points: You are a boxing maven. 5-20 points: You are a boxing scholar. 0 points: You are so much better off.

—ESPN.com, January 25, 2002

MUHAMMAD
ALI

The profound grace with which Muhammad Ali faced the effects of Parkinson's disease only enhanced Wiley's opinion that he was "one of the five greatest men to draw breath in my lifetime." In this brief essay from Serenity, *he reflects on the man who shook up his world.*

Boxing is an art of self-defense. In order to refine and exhibit this art, one must fend off attack. The more powerful the attack, the more resourceful the boxer must be to overcome it. Often the best defense is a good offense. At times, in fact quite frequently, the attack is so relentless that a boxer is knocked down, out, or dead.

Over a twenty-year span, the body and head of Muhammad Ali were laid siege to by such plunderers as Sonny Liston, George Foreman, Ken Norton, Earnie Shavers, and the remorseless Joe Frazier. Ali spent some 102 three-minute rounds, some five solid hours, fending off these men, buffeted by what amounted to a seventy-three-inch fist.

After seeing Ali endure this, and much more, did we really need an anonymous British neurologist to tell us that the champion has suffered brain damage?

This is better than *The Emperor's New Clothes*.

Damage, specifically brain damage, is what boxing is all about. Boxing is assault and battery with deadly weapons called the fists of man. Ali's brain could not possibly be the same as before he entered the ring, and Ali was a pitcher. Think of the catchers, the guys who took three to give one, the crowd pleasers, the club fighters, the meat, the stiff, the tomato cans, the ham-and-eggers.

Boxing is full of brain damage. Ali seemed untouchable. But he has urinated blood after a fight, had his jaw broken, felt his face tighten as it swelled to twice normal size, been knocked on his can, battered his hands beyond repair, and suffered several concussions. After fighting Frazier for fourteen rounds in Manila in 1975, he said, "It's the closest thing to death that I know of." Maybe people have deluded themselves. Maybe they think boxers beat each other for fifteen rounds and come out ready for a set of doubles or a movie premiere.

Have you ever wondered at the miracle of a cauliflower era or a nose warped in three directions? Do you know what a smashed Adam's apple feels like? How long it takes for a shattered cheekbone to heal? Do you know what it's like not being able to wait for that cheek to heal properly before getting in the ring again? How it feels to have a ruptured sinus cavity drain into that cheek? Think this is some kind of game? Ever hear of Frankie Campbell, Jimmy Doyle, Benny Paret, Cleveland Denny, Willie Classen, or Duk Koo Kim?

What would you think if you couldn't get out of bed in the morning because of a traumatized liver? Can you imagine having your jaw broken and not going immediately to the hospital, but instead fighting for ten more rounds? Can you imagine hearing the man in front of you being exhorted to blast you on that jaw? Can you imagine not being able to reason with him, other than with your fists? Can you imagine thousands of your fellow humans screaming for your blood? Can you imagine the look on your mother's face while all this is happening? Brain damage, indeed.

Muhammad Ali's mother could tell you he's not the same man without consulting Great Britain about it. So could his longtime camp followers, only they might not admit it, even to themselves, because they'd rather see him as he was than as he is. This is no indictment of the system, the participants, or the viewers. This is just an expression of amazement at the world's naive and detached view of a prizefighter's eventual lot. If you fight for twenty years, you're lucky if all you end up with is slurred consonants and a memory that blinks. Yes, Muhammad Ali has suffered brain damage. But not one percent of the brain damage he has dished out. You see, none of them ever really wins.

The last time I saw Muhammad Ali was in the spring of 1987, after I left Ray Robinson for the last time. He was in the United Airlines terminal at the Los Angeles International Airport, sitting on a long seat of plastic cushions, near the windows, in the sun. He was alone and not sad about it. I did a double take. I had never seen him alone before. His traveling companions had probably gone to make sure of some arrangements. Ali sat there in dark glasses, unbothered, looking straight ahead. Serene.

I made his acquaintance again.

"Hello, Champ. You're looking good."

He smiled and said "Thank you, thank you," and offered his right for an even handshake. I bent over to accept, moved as ever. As we shook, the jacket I was carrying slipped off my shoulder.

"Whoops"—but I hardly had time to get it out of my mouth. Quicker than I can describe it, Ali's right released my hand and caught the jacket well before it reached my waist. He even smoothed it out for me. Reflexes. "Thanks, Champ."

Ali is an immense man, and nothing is more imposing than that great, handsome lion's head. I thought about the news of the day and the day before. Ali is going to the other board members at Kmart, wanting answers because the store wouldn't stock his shoe polish. Kinshasa. The Ali car. I'd never seen one. Manila. And, soon, the brain surgery Ali would consider, and later, other treatments. One doctor thought it might be exposure to pesticides that left Ali's tongue less supple, his brain less sharp. *"I shook up the world!"* The Parkinson's disease. *"I am the greatest!"* The numbing. *"I'm a baad man!"* He was only forty-five. He was not old enough to be my father.

I stood there next to him, saying nothing. I thought about asking him if Sugar Ray Leonard could beat Marvin Hagler. But then I knew what he would say to that. *Ali KO's Liston. Ali KO's Foreman . . . Float like a butterfly, sting like a bee . . . Rumble, young man, rumble . . .* I knew. So I held myself back. We had nothing but time. I told him, "You're one of the five greatest men to draw breath in my lifetime." He didn't say anything to that. He merely kept on smiling. So I smiled back and gained strength from the peaceful moment. Then I went on about my business.

—*From Serenity: A Boxing Memoir, 1989*

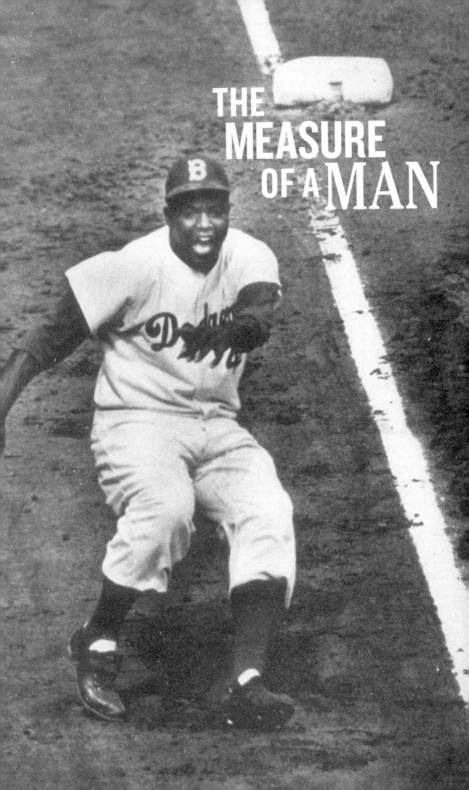

THE
MEASURE
OF A MAN

ON THE NATURAL SUPERIORTY
OF BLACK ATHLETES

In the late 1980s, CBS sports analyst Jimmy "the Greek" Snyder and Los Angeles Dodgers executive Al Campanis made very public comments about the dominance of black athletes. Never one to shy away from a good debate, Wiley weighed in with this spirited 1989 essay in Emerge *magazine.*

Are black people, all people of African descent but especially African-American men, naturally superior athletes? If you are asking me, I'd have to say, not that I've noticed. But why ask in the first place? I want to know why black men have to be naturally superior athletes. If we are, it would inevitably follow that black men are naturally inferior at something else. Like thinking. Trust me. If not me, trust history. Go back to Germany fifty years ago. Go back a hundred years, to the Trail of Tears toward Oklahoma. Go to South Africa next weekend. It follows black people are not quite . . . right. Not quite . . . human.

So the question becomes why ask? Ego? Sour grapes? More? This is no choice, and I'd rather not see it reach that point, so I will attempt to shatter the theory of racial athletic superiority with an expert exhibition of word-processor boxing. I'm going to set you up, then hit you with the clincher.

First, some particulars:

Jimmy "the Greek" Snyder was at Duke Zeibert's restaurant in Georgetown in January 1988, just as Doug Williams was about to play quarterback for the Washington Redskins in the Super Bowl. Snyder intimated that black people were better athletes because they had been bred to be that way, with large thighs which shot up into their backs.

On a *Nightline* interview from Houston in the spring of 1987, Al Campanis, an executive with the Los Angeles Dodgers, said he believed black people lacked "the necessities" to be field or general managers. "How many are good swimmers?" he asked. "Or pitchers?" Somewhere, three men named Frank Robinson, Anthony Nesty, and Dwight Gooden weren't laughing. Here was institutional racism in the flesh, in all its suicidal, self-aggrandizing debasement.

Early in 1989, Tom Brokaw hosted an NBC program entitled "The Black Athlete: Fact and Fiction," then went on to utterly ignore the facts for the speculations of two scientists. Present in panel form were Dr. Harry Edwards, the Berkeley sociologist; Arthur Ashe, the author and former tennis champion; two scientists who were not named Mengele. Others, like baseball star Mike Schmidt and Olympian Carl Lewis, were heard from on videotape. This program accomplished one feat—it flushed out a certain . . .

Roger Stanton, publisher of pulp sports magazines, who wrote Brokaw a letter. And it was not a love letter. Stanton: ". . . . black players lack discipline, and they are the ones most likely to get into trouble . . . . [A] black player in general pays less attention to such things as showing up on time or following a rigid routine . . . .

[Edwards's] contention that blacks turn to athletics because they cannot do well in other professions is ridiculous. They can be lawyers, doctors, or businessmen if they so desire. But it takes hard work and discipline, and in many instances they are not willing to pay the price . . . . Quarterback is a very intricate position and there are not many blacks qualified . . . . If you gave twenty white college players an IQ test, the whites would outshine the blacks every time."

We can strike Snyder and Campanis. You could nearly understand them. They were old, fat with the kill, and drunk or getting there. Television cameras and reporters Ed Hotaling and Ted Koppel happened to show up at the wrong time for them. Stanton was ignorant, which would be fine, except he had the forum to disseminate his ignorance. He undoubtedly kowtowed to journalism's double standard regarding black and white athletes. A middle-aged black former athlete "overdoses on drugs," and his immoral carcass is laid open on journalism's streets. A middle-aged white former athlete "has a heart attack of undetermined cause" and we are told how much he loved children. Stanton also wrote that Doug Williams's brilliant performance in the 1988 Super Bowl "may have been a fluke." Stanton is inaccurate here. Make that four flukes. In one quarter. On one leg.

But why would a sober sort like Brokaw enter this debacle? His program, while it attempted seriousness, played like a badly tuned farce. Here the doctors were advancing the fast-twitch, slow-twitch muscle theory which states that black people from a certain region of Africa (they can't make up their minds if it is East or West Africa) and their more immediate descendants are better at explosive sports, sprints in track, short distances, hoop, while Europeans have slow-twitch muscles which enable them to win the longer races. This came after an Olympics where white men had won the gold medals in basketball and volleyball, which are quite explosive sports.

Meanwhile, blacks from Kenya dominated the long-distance races out on the track, and later Ethiopians dominated the Boston Marathon and world cross-country championships. The Russian Valery Borzov, a white man, won the Olympic gold medal in hundred meters in 1972. The Russians won the four-by-hundred-meter relay in 1988 as well. And the world two-hundred-meter record holder is not Carl Lewis, but an Italian, of all people, Pietro Mennea. No one on Tom Brokaw's special brought this up, least of all the doctors, who were too busy admitting they were testing the muscle fibers in all these cute little children's legs.

It was weird.

Then came the tape of Mike Schmidt, saying he would have to agree that black men seem to have the edge as natural athletes. I guess they never had any mirrors in the clubhouse of the Philadelphia Phillies, for whom Schmidt toiled so long and so well. Mike Schmidt is only the greatest third baseman in the history of Major League Baseball. Lots of black men have played third base in the major leagues since Jackie Robinson broke the color line. Yet Schmidt still thinks black men are naturally superior athletes. He'd always wanted to slam-dunk, but he could only hit 548 home runs in the Show. Poor Schmitty.

Then came Carl Lewis, who said black athletes seemed to be "made better." Carl can be narcissistic. If he was Serbo-Croatian, they would be "made better," no doubt. Ashe said, "My head tells me yes, but my heart tells me no," or vice versa, on the question. The greatest victory of Ashe's career came at Wimbledon in 1975, when he defeated Jimmy Connors. By this time, Connors, who is white, was quicker and hit harder than Ashe. Connors was, in fact, the number one player in the world. But Ashe out-thought him, refusing to play power against power. Ashe moved the ball around, gave Connors nothing to feed off, and won on guile as much as athletic ability. But his heart said no and his head said yes, or vice versa. Ashe had recently completed a compendium entitled *The History of the Black Athlete*, so I assume he was caught up in his subject matter.

Many older black people subscribe to the theory that black men are naturally superior athletes. No way you can convince them otherwise. There are reasons for their attitude. Before integration of sports in this country (which came after the aberration of Jack Johnson, and began in the boxing ring with Joe Louis and in baseball with Jackie Robinson), all the testimonials were that black people were naturally *inferior* athletically, as in everything else. Black men could not develop the mental discipline it took to go fifteen rounds, or play second base in a taut, 2-1 World Series game.

Blacks wouldn't work hard enough. Athletics had a mental side then, and a work-ethic side. Mentally, ethically, black men could accomplish nothing without a white man behind them with a whip. That was what was publicized, and thus became the apparent consensus.

Then along came Joe Louis, knocking out the apparent consensus, represented by Max Schmeling, a strong boxer who through no fault of his own happened to be employed by one Adolf Hitler. So even many white people got behind Joe. But all along the white people had Tarzan, the Green Hornet, Superman, Batman, movie stars, presidents, publicized aviators, and captains of industry. Having escaped the shackles of slavery a bare seventy-five years, black people had *Birth of a Nation* and *Amos 'n' Andy* as the total publicized cultural reparations. Financial reparations were not forthcoming. In this kind of hostile environment, as you might imagine, Joe Louis became Tarzan, the Green Hornet, Superman, Batman, movie stars, etc., all rolled into one. Joe dared not lose. Lose, in the one place where the field was almost level? Out of the question.

Recently I was a victim on *Tony Brown's Journal*, where a debate was raised on this thorny issue. I explained that in boxing, for example, the fighters had come from poor backgrounds. Fighting was their last resort. That's why they were good at it. After the taping, a well-dresed middle-aged black man came up to me and said, "Michael Jordan's parents weren't poor. So how do you explain Michael Jordan?"

I laughed and told the man that I really couldn't blame anybody for watching Michael Jordan play basketball and thinking he was not quite human. But then I said, "Did you know he was once cut from his high school basketball team?" And then I said, "You know, just because Air Jordan is the best basketball player on earth, that is no reflection on you. All the credit goes to Mikey, hard work, and God."

From Barbara Turpin, Ph.D., assistant professor of psychology at Southwest Missouri State University: "There is a sociological side to the belief that genetics is the sole cause of black athletic superiority and white intellectual ability. Whites can say, 'Well, of course I'm not like Isiah Thomas; I don't have the genes,' or blacks can say, and I've heard my black students say it, 'Well, of course I can't get a doctorate; I don't have the genes for it.' It allows people to avoid taking responsibility for their own behaviors. And a genetic determination argument allows racism to have a scientific basis, and justified the denial of opportunity to the 'inferior' group."

Dr. Alvin Poussaint, psychiatrist, consultant to *The Cosby Show*, among others, describes it as a "dangerous theory." He says, "In some whites there is an unwillingness to face the fact that black athletes work harder . . . . Throughout the years of discrimination, blacks began to see sport as survival. You do what you've been trained to do. But along the way, the traits which made [them] able to excel at sports—mental acuity, mental concentration, mental toughness, work ethic—the very traits blacks weren't supposed to have and supposedly were the reason to keep them out of sports in the first place, now those traits are given little or no credence. Why don't we look at the mental work within the sport? . . . . If the attitude of the majority and minority were more open, more blacks would become mathematicians and scientists. Right now, it's a matter of a self-fulfilling prophecy."

To those black students who don't think they have the genes for doctorates, know that black people invented a few things, even without a Batman to inspire them. When you talk about the real McCoy, you are not talking about Walter Brennan, but about Elijah McCoy, who was an inventor of train engine lubrication systems, not a Green Bay Packer running back.

So here is the most immediate negative ramification of the black athlete theory. It stunts and denudes black men, who are the largest virtually untapped natural resource left in this country, at a time when it needs its resources.

Once I had a conversation with Howie Long, the All-Pro defensive lineman of the L.A. Raiders. Long, who is white, was raving over John Elway, the All-Pro quarterback of the Denver Broncos. John Elway is white, too. After saying how great Elway was, Long told me, "You know, Ralph, he plays like a brother." I raised my eyebrows. Howie said, "Here comes that brother shit." I gently reminded him he brought up brothers. I hadn't. Howie paused, then looked as though somebody had hit him in the face with an ax handle.

A white former colleague of mine likes to point out that the Chinese consider themselves athletically inferior to whites and far inferior to blacks. Well, not all Chinese. The world high-jump record holder at seven-foot-ten was a tall man from China. Did he Zen his way over the bar, or what? The greatest female track athlete I ever saw was Chi Chen, also Chinese. For flexibility and versatility, Chen made Florence Griffith-Joyner look like, well, a girl. Michael Chang, the seventeen-year-old second generation Chinese-American, did not win the 1989 French Open because the epicanthic folds of his eyes helped him see the ball better, did he?

The games belong to the people who play them well.

Some of these players were white men like Bill Walton, Valery Brumel, Jerry West, John Havlicek, Tom Chambers, Mark McGwire, George Case, Rex Chapman, Terry Bradshaw, Joe Montana, Dick Butkus, Max Baer, Pete Maravich, Hugh McElhenny, Paul Westphal, Dave Cowens, Bob Lilly, Bruce Jenner, Will Clark, Bobby Jones, Bob Mathias, Roger Staubach, Billy Cunningham, Don Hutson, Glenn Davis, Babe Ruth, Ted Williams, Ty Cobb, Mickey Mantle, Cal Ripken, Jr., Boris Becker, Sergei Bubka, Lance Alworth, Joe DiMaggio, Bronko Nagurski . . . say, this is getting boring, isn't it?

You might say some of these not-quite-human athletes are no longer playing. What has that to do with it? Did all white people stop being able to play once a few retired? Or did the attitudes change when America noticed most athletic heroes were black?

Boxing is the clincher. It is the purest form of sport, one man trying to stop another, and defending himself. It is not for the faint of heart or the satisfied. In the early part of this century, there were great Irish boxers, great Jewish boxers, great Italian boxers, but hardly any of those exist anymore because they have found assimilation work and in many cases good fortune. Work and good fortune are more reliable than boxing. Now, and most assuredly all along, there have been great black boxers. Does this mean all blacks are naturally superior boxers, because they still do it? Only if you're not paying attention.

By way of example, I offer the June 12, 1989, fight to a draw between Sugar Ray Leonard and Thomas "Hit Man" Hearns.

In my opinion, Leonard and Hearns are two of the greatest prizefighters of this era. They are in their early thirties now, so a lot of talk was going around that they shouldn't be fighting. They were washed up. Well, of course they shouldn't have been fighting, but where else could two black men earn $24 million in one night? On June 12, they fought back and forth, taking turns hurting each other with brilliant exhibitions of the science, for twelve brutal rounds. There is a young boxer named Michael Nunn—black, of course—who is in the same weight class as Leonard and Hearns. Much is made of what he will do to them one day. And I have no doubt he shall. But if he had been in that ring on June 12, against either Hearns or Leonard, Nunn would have been knocked out, because these two champion boxers went beyond mere athletic skill.

Hearns knocked Leonard down in the third round, beating him to the draw as they both threw rights. Leonard had decided to go for Hearns early with a lightning right lead. But Hearns was up to the mark for it and threw his at the same time and it was a question of landing most correctly, in the most debilitating fashion. It was a question of inches, and for that split second, Hearns was a better problem-solver. Leonard went down a few missed punches later after that right caught him flush on the button of his chin. Leonard got up. He came back and hurt Hearns with a three-punch combination in the fifth. Hearns wobbled around the ring, tying Leonard up to survive. Leonard pinned him on the ropes, looking for the clincher. But Hearns threw a sharp left hook to Leonard's body, which made Ray reconsider. Hearns made it to the end of the round and stumbled back to his corner.

Emanuel Steward, Hearns's trainer-manager and another black man, kneeled in front of Hearns as he sat on the stool in the corner. Steward did not yell, or try to tell Hearns what he had done wrong. Steward said, "This is what makes a great fighter. This is what's going to make you great. Do you understand me, Tommy?" Hearns shook away the fog and nodded. He understood. There was nothing Steward could tell Hearns about boxing—Hearns is the world champion, not Steward.

But Steward could tell Hearns about life, about what it takes to live it well, to survive. To do this, he would have to come back from being hurt. I can guarantee you, the average middle-class black or white would have at this point said, "Well, that's enough of that," and asked Steward to cut his gloves off. Because to the average middle-class man, this would be the way to survive.

Hearns went out and hurt Leonard some more. In the seventh round, a quick left hook off the jab, a punch Hearns wasn't supposed to have, took Sugar Ray by surprise and only Ray's keen, learned talent for slipping punches took him through to the end of the round. Leonard was the best boxer alive at the time. Now he drew from within himself, his past. He went back and hurt Hearns and continued hurting him until the eleventh round. Hearns had been using his left, and had gotten Ray's attention. Hearns hardly threw the right. Ray hurt Hearns badly at the end of the ninth round, and in the tenth. But while hurting Hearns, he was disregarding the man's right more and more. Between the tenth and eleventh rounds, Steward told the truth in a boxing sense. "Throw your right hand, Tommy!" he beseeched. "They're begging you to throw the right hand! The right hand will take you home, Tommy!"

Leonard came into the eleventh looking for a knockout. A sleepy-looking Hearns casually measured him with the outstretched left jab. Briefly, Leonard may have considered the left hook Hearns used in the fifth and seventh rounds. He never saw the right. I videotaped this and ran the sequence back frame by frame. In one frame, Hearns's right was cocked, his left measuring Leonard. In the next frame, Hearns has already followed through with the right. It has already landed, and Leonard has been hurt. If that's washed up, I'm the Duke of Windsor. Leonard, hurt badly, was down a few punches later. But by sheer will, by mental capacity alone, he rose up, and by the end of the round was back in Hearns's chest, firing with both hands.

Leonard won the twelfth round going away. They refused to buckle, wilt, die. The will they displayed was palpable. At ringside, a white man, Jim Lampley, a broadcaster for HBO, said "You will seldom see a greater display of what it is that makes men fighters." His colleague, Larry Merchant, said "This had nothing to do with [boxing]; this had to do with what these two men are made of." And if Jim Lampley and Larry Merchant never say another mouthful, they did then.

Later, after I left Las Vegas, I was riding in a rough part of East Oakland, California, with a friend. We passed a corner where three or four young boys were standing. One of the boys was eleven or twelve, and he had decided to pick on another boy, who seemed to be about nine. They were both thin, poorly dressed, unkempt, and of African descent. The bigger boy ran around the smaller boy and wrapped him in a bear hug. Then he quickly punched the smaller boy in the head with a right. Hard. Not like television. Real. The older boy performed his coward's trick again, and again. After the third hard right to the head, the smaller boy bounced away from the bigger boy, enraged. He pumped his fist almost happily. The older boy looked at him and something changed in his eyes. And then my friend, who was driving, turned the corner. Now some people might say, "Well, you two are grown men. Why didn't you stop them?" Those are the same people who might ask if black men are naturally superior ath-letes. "So now the little kid won't have to fight again tomorrow," I said to my sober friend, who nodded knowingly. He is also a black man who has a son. "Either that or he'll have a very tough skin by the time he's eighteen," he said. I nodded back.

Now if this is what you want to call the natural athletic superi-ority of the black male athlete, then so be it for you. Some of us call it survival, though.

Them rights hurt.

—*Emerge, March 1989*

THE QUIET WAR
OF TONI SMITH

When Manhattanville College basketball player Toni Smith turned her back on the flag during several National Anthems in 2003, her silent protests drew boisterous media attention. Unlike most, who saw Smith's actions as unpatriotic, Wiley compared the twenty-one-year-old sociology major's statement to another famous Smith, Tommie, who along with John Carlos gave the black power salute on the medal stand at the 1968 Olympics.

The question before us is if the sporting arena is the proper venue for airing social protest, whether athletes involved in sports are proper messengers of political conscience.

It depends on who you are. If you're just a jock, looking to maintain that comfortable, peculiar but undeniable societal status that goes along with being a jock, then you don't want that peculiar status threatened. If you're a fan, you come to sports not to think about "stuff like that." But if you're an actual living, breathing human being, on whom education was not wasted, you follow your conscience.

In the end, it's not important what others think of you.

It's what you think of yourself.

There are no rules about how to express this, except, one hopes, that you'd do it lawfully, peacefully, and effectively.

I'd say Toni Smith has figured this out better than most.

Two million hits on a once-lonely Manhattanville College Web site says the Quiet War of Toni Smith has been effectively trans-mitted out to the world. This was not her intent, to become TV programming, to become debate material for the rest of us. She is a twenty-one-year-old sociology major who stands facing away from the American flag during the playing of the pre-game National Anthem before her collegiate games. Big deal. She did not begin doing this for notoriety. It was her quiet, private expression to herself of her own thoughts, her own ideas, and moral judgments.

Things you'd want your own twenty-one-year-old daughter to do.

Her statement has been picked up, not by her, but by us, as the latest "controversy," cause celebre, political football; it makes her a pariah in some quarters, as the nation careens towards war. Reminds me in a way of 1968, a volatile year in which Martin Luther King Jr. and Robert Kennedy were killed, the body bags were coming back to Dover en masse as the war in Vietnam was going full tilt—and we still held the Olympics in Mexico City any-way, late that summer.

So where else would you protest? Wherever you are.

We've all seen the pictures of Tommie Smith and John Carlos standing on the medal podium in black-stockinged feet, with their fists raised in a black-gloved salute. They were saying essentially what Toni Smith is saying—people have died, people are dying, not all of them by noble means or for noble ends, and when will it end?

It must all end.

Mustn't it?

Well, actually, it doesn't have to, it never does, and social progress is made grudgingly, if at all, a precious inch at a time, just as the envelope of human endeavor is stretched in athletics, an inch at a time. When you are young, you want it to change all at once. It never does. Vengeance is mine, sayeth the Lord.

But what Toni Smith doesn't know, and I hope to God she never does, is that very often these protests end with the ostracizing of the protestors rather than the evils they protest. It is a testimony to Tommie Smith and John Carlos that they managed to survive being "blacklisted" from any work, a simple job, for the next 25 years, much less being tossed from the Olympic Games.

Toni Smith doesn't deserve that, nor, frankly, is she likely to have to endure it. She'll move on, and maybe she'll change and grow to accept Status Quo.

I hope to God she doesn't. I hope she always remembers.

Young people who major in sociology ask questions about historical matters like the 1968 Olympic Games or the 1936 Olympic Games or the 1972 Olympic Games or the Trail of Tears or any of a thousand atrocities and the many wars that continue to occur. Young people who major in sociology are given pause once they learn and process the bloody history of this or any other "civilized" country.

We live, love, learn. Even if we are athletes. Imagine that. To say athletes and sports are precluded from this process is, in fact, insulting, that a Tommie or a Toni Smith are like cattle and should just give their milk and moo and shut up and not have their own feelings. We should be proud of them. What they are doing is actually an act of love.

But we're not proud of them. I shouldn't say "we," because some of us are proud of them, or at least tolerant of their opinions. That's what all those people died for; freedom, tolerance, not cloth flags.

Just Tuesday in Orlando, Florida, a fossil of a man named Pete Barr, an out-and-out bigot known for spewing invective against blacks, Jews, women, and everybody else within maximum effective range, without a mention of any of them ever being American, or patriots, lost in the city's mayoral race, but by only 5,000 votes. Over 17,000 people voted for his opponent, Buddy Dyer—but over 12,000 voted for Barr. That's Sociology 101, too.

Yes, Toni, at times it's enough to make you turn away. But we all, including Toni Smith, have the precious right to vote; and the vote is the greatest social protest—and right—of them all. On some issues you don't get to post a ballot. In that case, you use the only bullet that should be used on another person—one's own conscious act of social protest.

But most of us seem to despise athletes for even thinking in the first place. So a grey-haired man named Jerry Kiley, who said he was a Vietnam veteran, ran onto the court with an American flag, ran right up to Toni Smith, seemingly as if to make her flinch, shrink away, to scream at her, to tell her she, not him, was a disgrace, to intimidate her.

Now was that admirable? Why? Who seemed cowardly? Who's the real red-blooded American in that picture, the athletic girl with a questioning mind and big heart who put her hands on her hips and stood there unafraid, or the old man running up to a young girl to try and bully her, his true intentions, his inner motivations, all covered up, wrapped inside and hidden away in an American flag? You tell me.

Toni Smith's statement was brief. To acknowledge those who have died for the country, you have to acknowledge those who died to claim it, then build it up. Agree or disagree with her method of illustration, her point is still lucid, logical, well-taken, and at the end of the day, irrefutable. Life will teach her its lessons. But she was born with the freedom to speak up. To tell her to shut up because she's "wrong," or because she's an athlete, or because this isn't the proper venue or time only increases the hypocrisy.

She's a smart girl. She knows this.

It's people like quiet Toni Smith, or quiet Tommie Smith, or quiet tennis champion Arthur Ashe, picketing outside of a South African embassy during the reign of apartheid, who give us the conscience and the respect we so often lack.

I don't feel Toni Smith isn't patriotic, or doesn't love America. In fact . . . well, my own words and talents are inadequate to explain what I sense here, so I will leave it to a better essayist than me. James Baldwin once wrote this:

"Societies never know it, but the war of an artist (or athlete) with a society is a lover's war, and (s)he does, at (her) best, what lovers do, which is to reveal the beloved to himself, and, with that revelation, to make freedom real . . . ."

—*ESPN.com, February 28, 2003*

W.W.J.D.?

Frustrated with too many punks in the NBA, too few minorities in the front office and coaching, and the general decline of respect in sports, Wiley asked this eternal question in a 2003 ESPN.com column: "What Would Jackie Robinson do?"

Whenever a choice of actions, reactions, or just a fork in the road confront today's black athletes, they should all pause, then ask themselves one question: "What would Jackie Robinson do?"

If he could come back from being dead and gone for thirty-one years, the first thing he'd do is shake somebody's hand in baseball until it made a splintering sound and the guy drew back a nub. Bud Selig would be as good a place as any to start, but I get the feeling Jackie would be passing out handshakes all around. For it is the NFL, pro and college football, and not baseball, that trails in society, in its minority hiring practice for field managers or head coaches. It is the NBA and college basketball, not baseball, which needs lessons in self-control, discipline, manhood—or a shot to the teeth. Jackie Robinson was adept at passing out all three lessons.

About twenty-three percent of big-league field managers are minorities. It would be important to Jackie to make sure they were the right men. As the late Justice Thurgood Marshall said, "A black snake is just as bad as a white snake." Jackie would try to make sure snakes in protestor clothing didn't get hired and

225

muck up the works for the real deserving minority candidates who could be out-and-out great managers and coaches. You don't just go grab the first black guy you see and stick him in there— unless for some reason you don't want to see him get the job done right in the first place.

Jackie would start a consulting clearinghouse where he and his staff's steely-eyed personal interviews would determine if a head coaching or managerial candidate had the goods, or was just riding on someone else's coattails.

Some thirty-seven percent of head coaches in the NBA are minority, in this case, African-American. Jackie Robinson would say, "That's how it should be, isn't it? Coaches in the NBA are not what I want to talk about. I want to talk about a–holes."

As for all these would-be Thugs and Killers in the NBA, waiting for people in parking lots and by loading docks and near benches, wanting to throw hands and sling lead, like they are all answering casting calls for revivals of *West Side Story*, or *Colors* . . . all that trash-talking and beating on their chests, Jackie would have two words them:

"Try me."

"Try me, sucker, tough guy, front-runner. Try me, after I've given up the better part of my life and all of my old age by holding in my righteous anger and rage at really deserving subjects who were trying to hurt me, and keep me from making a living, and keep me from making a future for you or your children, a future that you in your malignant ignorance are now screwing up royally for those who follow you. You think the world owes you a living, jerk? Don't you know anything, fool-ass boy? Who died and made you Prince of Mid-Air? If it weren't for me, you'd be jumping over dog poop in the backyard for free. Think being rich is your divine and selfish right, clown? Yes, you, you're nothing but a clown. A weak, stupid clown. And you're actually dangerous. Dangerous to yourself, to your family, and to my legacy. And if you don't like it, Mills, Rasheed, Ron Artest, then come get some."

You think the NBA bullies would be offended? Probably. Just about everything offends them, when they are not abusing women or the refs. Then they'd be offended again, by Jackie Robinson picking them out for it, by everything except their own selfish acts of cruelty and disrespect, not only of authority but themselves and their peers. We know where the underlying hate comes from—the jealousy, the envy, and the long history of scientific bigotry as moral backbone for economic exploitation. That part's easy to figure, Jackie would think. Not really all that easy to deal with, but at least familiar. At least there is nobility in a fight against such evil. But where did all this self-hate come from? Where is the nobility in that? I think Jackie Robinson would think about that long and hard, and curse the men who left these babies to grow up into giants who don't know how to be men. He might blame music. He might blame movies. But, mostly, Jackie would blame them. Jackie would say, "You're not a man. You're a punk."

In retort, think the NBA or NFL bullies would want some of

227

Jackie Robinson bare-knuckled? I can pretty much guarantee you—not.

Not after they saw what he could do. They had to discharge Lt. Jackie Robinson out of the Army, you know. He kept beating the crap out of people who had disrespected him or his mission. They mustered him out for the good of the service. It was either that or drop him on Berlin or Tokyo, then duck and cover. Jackie's wife and partner, Rachel, was a nurse. Good thing, too.

You didn't want any of that—believe me. I don't know if even Chuck Bednarik, Jim Brown, Paul Bunyan, Sonny Liston, Luca Brasi, and Bill the Butcher put together would want any of that. In fact, I know they wouldn't. They'd have too much respect to try.

That's so much of what's missing today—respect. It's something that's not given. It must be earned. Only thing is, people are so confused today, they can't tell who has earned it or how.

Jackie could.

At heart, down deep, Jackie Robinson was pure football player. He even approached playing baseball that way. Today, only eight percent of head coaches in the NFL are minorities. Jackie would glower and fume about this and ask for a meeting and get it and odds are you wouldn't need Cochran & Mehri. I'd like to see the 49ers blow off Jackie Robinson.

Jackie would go to pro football mad today, because that's where a problem lies. He'd call for a Congressional hearing into the matter of both pro and college football hiring practices, where there are three black head coaches out of 117 at the

Division I-A level. But he'd start with pro football, because pro football today it is what baseball used to be when Jackie played. It is the revealer of the national character, it is the great national pastime, it is that which you'd better understand if you want to know America. It is the map of our hearts and minds.

Jackie would demand accountability, because the NFL is essentially operated like a public trust, with its own Congressional antitrust exemptions and taxpayer-financed superstadia initiatives holding up municipalities for millions of taxpayers' dollars. Jackie Robinson would demand some kind of accountability for this taxation without representation. His blood pressure would rise if remedies weren't forthcoming. That's what blinded and killed the mighty Jackie at fifty-three, hypertension and diabetes, a pounding in his veins, a deferred, internalized need and desire to see himself and his people (and yours) free to live, excel, or fail on their own merit.

Would Jackie Robinson have lived longer today, with better health care and meds, but still in this current climate of screed, dogma, diatribe, hate-eration, than he did live in helping to overcome the system of exploitive segregation? He'd probably live just long enough to ask the new national game of football some questions. Like, how in hell do you hire Dennis Erickson over Denny Green? Explain that to him.

Jackie would save some heat for the rank and file of the players.

Jackie would corner the playing population of all three major team sports in disgust, get in their faces; and you haven't been cornered until you've been cornered by Jackie Robinson. He'd want to know what the noise was about, what happened to wives, where discipline went. And since his own son died in an accident following a long bout with drug addiction, he'd have no patience with athletes who kept going out like that. If you want to get high, have the courtesy to do it on your own time, in the off-season, in Brazil or someplace. Interstate 5 after a road game is not the place to do it. That's what Jackie would say.

Jackie Robinson, who was born in Cairo, Georgia, back when a black man trying to be nothing but a man would be meant for a chain gang, if not death, would be surprised to see the SEC football teams now being populated mostly by young African-Americans, particularly young African-Americans who had no use for going to college. Jackie had been like that back at UCLA, and he was always sorry for it. He never saw a black SEC football player until the end, if he saw one then, in the era of the Bryants, Vaughts, Jordans, and Buttses. Black bodies on the field but none of their faces in coaching boxes or graduating classes would trouble him.

He'd wonder if they'd gone from cotton fields to playing fields. He wouldn't need Jesse Jackson to speak for him on it. He wouldn't abide Al Sharpton speaking for him on it. He'd be his own man.

He'd think the old, tried-and-true system of exploiting free labor was so advantageous to those receiving the fruits of those labors, that it would never change, not without a demand. Jackie Robinson would spit in a spluttering rage that zero African-

Americans had ever been head football coaches at taxpayer-driven, public state universities making up most of the SEC. "Unacceptable," he'd say.

Jackie Robinson would demand an audience with all the university presidents. He'd have Myles Brand on speed dial. He'd make the NCAA think it stood for, "Need to Catch African-Americans."

Jackie Robinson was the shotgun in the marriage between black and white, and although many of us belittle that marriage until this day—looking at each other and rolling our eyes and saying, "Yeah, that's my *skank* old lady"—we enjoy it when we win a national title or a war or big-time profits with the help of "The Other One." If they were going to budge the university presidents' hearts and minds, the way Jackie and Branch Rickey did with American hearts and minds, then that's what it was going to take, someone with the character, the fire, the shoulders, the stomach, the heart of a Jackie Robinson.

Jack would be backed by some very powerful people. Tyrone Willingham is too busy coaching Notre Dame to meet with university presidents. But Jackie Robinson wouldn't be—not today. What's Michael Jordan's excuse? Busy shooting commercials for glorified flavored water?

Jackie Robinson would be the one guy who could make Jordan or Richard Williams or Earl Woods listen to him in rapt awe.

At the same time, Jackie would admire Jordan and Serena and Venus and Tiger to the nth degree for their on-field prowess. And when they were eventually resented and examined and their loyalties tested, as his were, Jackie would tell them it's no big thing, and to keep going, to be true to themselves, to their country, and to what's right. Jackie never put the cart before the horse. He always knew nobody would care what he said, thought, or believed until he had given them a reason to, until he'd shown his skill, talent, tenacity, fearlessness, durability, and ability to win and be a team player on the field over time. You don't make an icon over the weekend. That's when people paid attention to him, over time. He'd get that across to Tiger.

Jackie Robinson would have zero tolerance for the malingerers, the guys who get their big-contract and sit there practicing their excuses while waiting for the next limo. He'd dismiss weak black coaches quicker than Sgt. Waters dismissed Pvt. Memphis.

Yes, Jackie would be cold to any inferior black coaches who thought getting a job via protest was the end of the line. "We can't afford you," Jackie would say, echoing Sgt. Waters in *A Soldier's Story*. They were no different than the inferior white coaches who thought getting a job via inheritance was the end of the line. Jackie would have pink slips and resumes flying around so fast we'd all think it was a ticker-tape parade. Jackie would be the judge of who could coach. We could trust him. Who else?

In college basketball, Jackie Robinson would've taken that pistol from former Tennessee State basketball coach Nolan Richardson III and threatened to beat his teeth out with it. And he would have done it, too, if III didn't have his office cleared out inside a half-hour.

Jackie Robinson would nod his head knowingly at the people who call into the sports talk shows in Lexington and say they hope Tubby Smith gets beat by L'ullville in the national championship game—just so they can get rid of him. Jackie would nod because he knows the intractability of racism. He could see how well the Kentucky team, featuring five black starters and a black coach, played the beautiful game, the team passing game of basketball. Jackie would call up Tubby and tell him the UCLA job was better; Jack could get Tub interviewed.

But Jackie would have never left baseball alone for long.

Jackie would say, "Put Pete Rose's ass in the Hall of Fame; you hypocritical S.O.B.s! A lot of people didn't want me in the Hall, either; my 'crime' was that my skin was black. That too was a crapshoot. I had no idea what color I'd be before I came out. I'm my mother's color. Got a problem with that?" If Jackie were to ask you that, I'd advise this answer: "No. No, sir. Not at all, sir."

Jackie would say that Vida Pinson and Frank Robinson and Curt Flood had good things to say about Pete, because he hung out on the wrong side of the dugout with them when they all were young, because he was from the wrong side of the tracks and some of his teammates—like Wally Post and big Klu—had no use for the kid. 4,196 hits later—let him in the Hall, Jackie would say. But don't let him back into organized baseball, because I saw from above where he screwed up the lineup card a few times, thereby disqualifying some of his hitters, and we can never con-

233

done compromising the integrity of the game.

Jackie would look around at Tony Pena in K.C., Jerry Manuel and Dusty Baker in Chicago, Frank Robinson in Montreal (and Puerto Rico), Lloyd McClendon in Pittsburgh ("Say, that's one of Pete's boys in Cincinnati, isn't it!"), and say that it was pretty good.

When Jackie gave his farewell address in what was then the new Riverfront Stadium in 1972, across town from Crosley Field where he had been booed and cursed and threatened as a black man trying to play a game of baseball in May of 1947, he said he dreamed of the day when he'd look out there and see those black managers.

So Jackie would be proud of baseball in that sense, in comparison to the NFL, and in the sense that baseball has progressed; a game once taught with such ignorance and blatant bigotry would have tried to pull itself up, to recognize that it was the one game that didn't discriminate, not in terms of national or continental origin or physical size or anything else. It was a game of skill, and of recognizing skills, and of deploying skills, and a black or brown man could do any of that as well as a white one. And vice versa.

Jackie Robinson would be the unofficial commissioner of baseball, in fact. He'd call up Sandy Koufax and Henry Aaron, and they would be his advisory committee. In fact, Jackie Robinson might be the unofficial czar of all sports. They gave the wrong guy the right name. It should have been Jackie "Mountain" Robinson.

His competitors called him Jackie "%#@&*!" Robinson.

But then, what would you expect? The side opposite of Jackie

Robinson isn't the black or white side. It's the wrong side.

Jackie would call up former Yankees GM Bob Watson and current ChiSox GM Kenny Williams. And Jackie would say to them and others who never had to go through the fire that he did, "You've got to replace yourselves with guys who can be like Mr. Rickey, who see the future, one possible future, and who see the inherent, intrinsic value in people. Don't let it stop with just you. ID the talent. Help it develop, then let it flow free."

That's what Jackie "%#@&*!" Robinson would do.

If Jackie Robinson were around today, I get the uneasy feeling that he would take one look around at the wide, wide world of sports, at what's been done, and undone, and what's left to do, and for all his strength, power, versatility, and relentlessness, I believe he'd start to cry. What I don't know is whether they'd be tears of joy or pain.

Probably both.

Then he'd do something.

—ESPN.com, March 4, 2003

FOOLS
RUSH IN

Fourteen years after Wiley's essay on the superiority of black athletes, radio talk show host Rush Limbaugh, appearing as a commentator on ESPN's Sunday NFL Countdown, remarked that Philadelphia Eagles quarterback Donovan McNabb was overrated because the media wanted a black quarterback to succeed. The ensuing controversy, during which Limbaugh resigned from ESPN, caused Wiley to offer some friendly advice.

How did we come to yet another "Yikes!" moment in NFL broadcast history? Who's guilty of what here in the Strange Case of Rush Limbaugh? The usual suspects are there: pride, ego, greed, power, hubris. But where does this episode stack up between Jimmy "The Greek" Snyder's lame and obtuse history lesson and Howard Cosell's "That little monkey!" naivete.

There was Rush Limbaugh, and then there he wasn't, resigning, quitting on his stool, so to speak. I wasn't glad about it. I wanted more. I wanted to hear Rush talk more football, just so I could laugh, and say, "What's my name?" while piling up the points in front of my friends and colleagues. I didn't want Rush to quit. I wanted him to stand in there and be forced to take it for the full twelve rounds. See how bad it would get—like when your friend keeps double-or-nothing raising against your pat straight flush.

It had seemed such an inspired move, hiring Rush in the first place, in the pure-numbers universe. Hard to move your number northward in today's cable universe—hey, let's bring Rush Limbaugh to ESPN's *Sunday NFL Countdown* team, along with Michael Irvin. Some matchup, huh? If that don't fetch 'em, I don't know Arkansaw! Or Florida. Or talk radio.

Along with the mainstays Chris Berman, Tom Jackson, and Steve Young, Rush would ride 'em, rope 'em, and brand 'em. And after three weeks, the ratings did bump up ten percent to a whopping 2.2 percent of the universe of 87.6 million households. Rush's last show drew a 2.4—not killer, but improved. But improved wasn't enough for Rushamon. He was going to take a big bite out of this apple. What you saw was ego beginning to run toward amok, not just on Rush's part either; yeah, ego is part of it, part of it everywhere and with everybody with few exceptions in this business, in my experience. Success, pure-numbers-wise, breeds ego. I'm just trying to explain it to you without prejudice. I'm not here to pile on Rush. No need. No room, anyway. I'm here to examine what he said, and in doing so examine the reaction to it.

It's a tricky thing, the peculiar anthropology known as professional sports expertise and knowledge. Espousing it is like any profession. Sure anybody can have an opinion and get it right one time in two. Or three. But it's the accumulation of knowledge, instinct, expertise, experience, gut feel, that gets you included among pro sports analysts. It's like baseball, in a way. For a game or two, or ten, a Triple-A'er can hang out with the big boys, when they are just clearing their throats, just getting in some swings, not going all out.

Anybody can pick winners on a pregame show, for a while; but that is not true professional knowledge, that is not noticing the telling nuance on the fly, bringing the little-known decisive moment or fact to life. It's what they pay people like me for. There's no other reason. It's not because they love me so much, or because they know I'll bring in a half-point's worth of ratings, and I don't believe that it's because I'm black, although you'd have to ask the media I work for. All I know for sure is, when the pro begins to apply his knowledge, in whatever occupation, then comes the separation. Just like what color you are, it's not something you look down and notice when working.

In the interest of full disclosure, let me say Rush Limbaugh e-mailed me as this pro-football season started, was complimentary of some things he'd read that I'd written about the NFL on Page 2. I e-mailed back, saying I was looking forward to hearing his take on the games, and that a truck driver had once told me, ten years ago, when I was out on tour with a non-sports book that was poorly titled *What Black People Should Do Now*—I was going for an ironic title there, but cut it too fine, and people read it literally, and thus the book failed—that he thought Rush and I had a lot in common (except for the key fact I didn't point out to the truck driver: Rush could afford a private jet, and I couldn't). One key here. I didn't tell Rush whether the truck driver had been white or black (he was white, but the telling point is, you were curious, weren't you?), because in this case, it shouldn't matter.

If only Rush had kept on e-mailing me, then I could have told him, "Not McNabb. Wrong dude. If you want to make that point, you should say . . ."

Rush was going along OK, picking winners and losers, giving opinions, just like anybody else who'd been lucky enough to be picked to be on an NFL pregame show. I ought to know. I've been there myself.

The first week, right out of the box, to prove himself, and establish his presence with authority, Rush picked a road dog, the Patriots to beat the Bills in Buffalo. The Bills won 31-0. The next week, Rush picked the Patriots to beat the Eagles in Philly. This time, New England won. So far, Rush is batting .500, (the pro analyst will bat .550—.750 in crunch-time—and there's the difference)—which is about like everybody else; hitting and missing, picking winners, giving opinions about who can play and who can't, and at which level the good player becomes mediocre. It was clear, at least to me, Rush had sources. (I know he had sources in and around the league; he mentioned consulting one of them about something I had once written about life at NFL training camp, whether or not it was authentic. This source told him it was, so Rush complimented me. The key here is Rush had to ask if it was authentic. I don't have to ask whether, say, *Playmakers* is authentic).

Here's where the lightning struck.

I'm just speculating now, but maybe it occurred to Rush, or to Rush's ego, on a completely logical level, as large egos begin to see logic, that he had not yet been Rush, that he hadn't yet made an appropriate impact. Rush is a mover and a shaker of public opinion, a big-number guy, a drink-stirrer; once he really starts rolling, being Rush, the viewership bump would really spike. The way he does that is by being controversial, plucking emotional strings.

Plus, Rush had a speaking gig coming up, delivering the keynoter to a gathering of broadcasters in Philly the first week of October—Thursday, October 2, to be precise. That would be four days after Rush said, "Sorry to say this, I don't think [McNabb] has been that good from the get-go; I think what we've had here is a little social concern in the NFL. The media has been very desirous that a black quarterback do well, black coaches and quarterbacks doing well. There is a little hope invested in McNabb, and he got a lot of credit for the performance of this team that he didn't deserve. The defense carried this team."

Rush, or his sources, or both, apparently don't think that much of the skills of McNabb. On the other hand, some people do. Jon Gruden, probably the top offensive talent evaluator in the league right now, raved about McNabb from that same get-go, the Senior Bowl of McNabb's senior year out of Syracuse. Gruden raved about what a great pro McNabb would be. Loved him. McNabb has since made Pro Bowls and twice played in the NFC Championship Game and two years ago finished runner-up as the MVP of the entire league. And he isn't even thirty years old.

Even in that ill-fated NFC title game loss, he was directing an inspired drive against the Tampa Bay defense, one of the best of all-time, until he threw a pick-and-go to Bucs cornerback Ronde Barber inside the Tampa Bay ten-yard line. McNabb has the skins on the wall, but that does not absolve him from critiques of his performance, informed or not.

The discussion was about like it is with all NFL quarterbacks, on balance, so far pretty normal. But it was the insertion of McNabb's race as a factor favoring his media coverage, and as a factor in the host institution (the NFL) and its reaction and support of McNabb, that was purely political. And that, not sports, is what Rush does to inflame the populace and bump his numbers. Period. That's what he does. So we can't act all surprised. Rush couldn't lay back and just be one of the boys talking ball and still be Rush. And he just had to be Rush. He had to try to turn it into an anti-affirmative action, hot-button debate about the liberal media that would inflame the part of the audience that expects such inflammation from him, and thrives on it.

Here's where the lack of football knowledge hurt Rush. His point could not be covered in a football sense, which made suspect his further speculation that the media and the league favored McNabb, and therefore all African-American quarterbacks. But, God help us, if he had chosen Kordell . . . .

Sunday NFL Countdown had suddenly become *Meet The Press*. Or maybe *Triumph of the Will*. Or at least of the Rush.

The Eagles were coming off a bye week, after looking pretty lame, McNabb included, in home losses to Tampa Bay and New England, not coincidentally the last two Super Bowl champion defenses. The 0-2 Eagles were going to Buffalo, itself coming off a loss to the Dolphins in Miami, no doubt looking to get well. And remember, the Bills had looked good that first week. And Rush has that speaking engagement coming up in Philadelphia. *Hmmmm . . . .*

In a perfectly logical marketing move, but perfectly naive football move, Rush went on the air and basically did what Rush does. He decided to do a power move, and use McNabb to make his point, figuring McNabb would be down in flames again, and Rush would not only be hotter on ESPN, but also in Philly to, you will forgive the expression, crow about it.

It was completely logical, not what he said, but the fact that Rush Limbaugh would say it. Completely logical—except for the football part, and the social part. What he said was, in fact, incorrect. I'm not talking about right and not right. Guys (and gals) are right and not right about football every weekend on ESPN. I myself think, for instance, Kurt Warner is overrated, but I am not going to add a theory that Warner is being propped up by the league and the St. Louis media because he is white. But would I, or anybody else, think it? Do we see ourselves and our own fates personified by who's under center? This is where Rush insinuates himself, into your less-than-better self. His point, if pressed, would be that he was talking about what's in the media's mind and hearts, which you can throw into question about basically anything.

Rush could have been content with staying with picking scores, evaluating performances, calling into question players' abilities, and helping *Sunday NFL Countdown* enjoy that ratings bump until the cows came home, and it would have been no problem. But, simply put, that wasn't enough for Rush. He had to be the bell cow. He calls into question McNabb's abilities and the intentions of the NFL and media covering it, pitting both against the white male majority, essentially, then sitting back and watching a bomb go off. He was incorrect, but people are incorrect in evaluating football players virtually all the time.

The only question is, was he correct about the "Social Concern" part?

The great thing about text, even in an audio/video sound-bite world, is that sometimes it's the only way to closely examine truth and falsehood.

Being correct has gotten a bad name, because all somebody has to do is shout "political!" in front of your correctness, and suddenly it's a bad thing.

Now if Rush had e-mailed me, I would've told him, "Rush, if you want to generalize about unspoken feelings about black quarterbacks, I'd advise against it. But, hey, you're you and you're gonna do what you're gonna do. I'd wait until I had a speaking gig in Chicago, if I were you, then you can question Kordell Stewart's abilities until your heart's content. At least you'll be right about the football part."

Even if Rush had kept reading his Page 2 R-Dub and Road Dog NFL columns (he probably did) he would at least have been delivered of the opinion that the Eagles were lacking in areas around and other than McNabb. But Rush didn't do that. Or worse, he did, and then flew in the face of it, rendering any prior compliments to me moot. He chose to go after Donovan McNabb and make him the anti-affirmative action baby.

Wrong guy. (Whew!)

McNabb was the wrong guy to pick. Or, the right guy to pick, if you don't have much of an agreement with Rush's methodology.

McNabb is the right/wrong guy for the same reason Jackie Robinson was the right/wrong guy. Among the best of the young African-American NFL quarterbacks—Steve McNair, Daunte Culpepper, Michael Vick, and McNabb—if we insist on breaking them down that way, McNabb might be the least QB-skills gifted among them, just as among Jackie Robinson, Henry Aaron, Willie Mays, and Roberto Clemente, Robinson might have been the least skilled as a baseball player. But Jackie was still plenty gifted enough to be a Hall of Famer. But he was even more, and I sense the same in McNabb. The others are accomplished (McNair has been to a Super Bowl, two AFC title games; Vick has already won a playoff game at Lambeau Field, something no other opposing quarterback has accomplished; Culpepper has been in an NFC title game), but not necessarily verbal. They cannot defend themselves in the clinches of little verbal political games nearly as well as they play football; they could not come back and spar with the likes of Rush or his quoted material being thrown in their faces for rebuttal. But it was no problem for

McNabb to rebut it.

"I'm sure he's not the only one who feels that way," McNabb astutely said in a news conference, a few days after surprising some, but not the people who really know pro football, by leading the Eagles to a 23-13 victory over Buffalo, and taking some of the steam out of Rush's stride. "But it's somewhat shocking to actually hear that on national TV." (So, McNabb had identified the nerve that Rush works for a living, admitted it was there, and then expressed shock one would let one's worse self be on public display.)

". . . . A free ride from the media in Philadelphia? That's a good one." (McNabb exposed Rush's lack of knowledge of sports media by locale, by reminding us that in Philly he had been booed on draft day, and that Philly fans boo everyone from Mike Schmidt to Santa Claus, let alone Donnie McNabb, and that the Philly press, like the New York press, only worse, treats every game outcome as if it were the pivotal battle for World War II, and if you lose, you're a bum.)

Let us crush two notions with one stone. First is the notion that quarterbacks are paragons of intelligence who hang in the pocket until the last minute to deliver passes in their down time from composing sonnets and concertos and writing motivational speeches for businessmen and splitting the atom. Oh, please. Really.

Four of the five best quarterbacks ever were Johnny Unitas, John Elway, Joe Montana, and Steve Young. Of the four, Unitas might have been the best football player. Definitely he would have scored the lowest on the SAT. There are mushrooms that would have scored higher on the SAT. Unitas was no genius. No book genius. No verbal genius. As far as being "pocket passers," the term is used for white quarterbacks in media; but that is simply the classic quarterback pose if that QB is on a team good enough to consistently form an impregnable pocket around him.

You can't be a pocket passer while the defense is sending sell-out blitzes at you. Then you must adapt, modify, improvise. Then you must play football.

Every great quarterback has been able to run, white or black, at one point or another, until they either got too old or too busted up to do so. This is football, people. These are not the wheelchair games. Unitas would be forty yards downfield flying in front of his ball-carrier running a reverse, throwing cross-body blocks. Fran Tarkenton must have run 200 miles behind the line of scrimmage alone. Montana ran like the wind. Elway was a runner, as was Young. This is no new phenomenon, because black quarterbacks do it.

What is relatively new is the spiked degree of difficulty of the position, with all the exotic blitzes and specialty edge rushers and size and speed of the defenders today. Charlie Ward, Heisman Trophy quarterback of Florida State and point guard on the Seminoles basketball team, decided to play in the NBA and forsake football, the game at which he had true genius, because of the beating required to play the position. "I've seen what happens," Ward said, alluding to several Florida State quarterbacks being grievously injured in practice while he was there. The rise and proliferation of black NFL QBs since Doug Williams won the Super Bowl in 1988 has more to do with the increased degree of difficulty of the position than any "social concern."

There are only a small number of people who can actually physically and mentally—like combat, it has more to do with fortitude and cunning than intelligence—play quarterback in the NFL. And there are not that many. There are more Ron Jaworskis of any color than John Elways of any color, with Elway being the standard of QB play.

To me, Steve McNair is the closest thing out there to the standard that is John Elway. We do find it interesting that Jaworski always says you must run the game from the pocket. It serves his own playing style and memory, his own persona and ego. That's exactly the feeling that Rush preyed upon. We all vicariously play through the people on the field on NFL Sundays—reflecting our own unique frame of reference. If they look like us, are we more likely to root for them?

Is there an undercurrent of false knowledge that does discriminate against the likes of a Peyton Manning? Again, to the trained eyes, and not even to every trained eye, but certainly to mine, Peyton Manning is a great quarterback. The fact that he has not won a playoff game—yet!—speaks more to the quality of the team around him than to Peyton. People say, "Yeah, he could never beat Florida when he was at Tennessee." Believe me, if Peyton had played for Steve Spurrier at Florida, or at Tennessee, they would have beaten Phil Fulmer at Tennessee, or Florida. But there is an undercurrent of false hipness and currency to a media perception about Peyton Manning's supposed shortcomings. Is it based on the color of his skin? Absurd, I know, but is it? That's what Rush was preying on.

You can have a pro like Kordell Stewart or a collegian like Carlyle Holliday, who either are too mechanical (Stewart) or have little or no feel for the position in the pro style (Holliday), but who are very mobile. And you can also be not the most mobile (Manning) and have a total feel for the position. Black and white have nothing to do with it. But do not think Peyton Manning is not a tremendous athlete. His father Archie was the best athlete I had seen at the position, before Elway came along. For some reason, even the Colts' own kicker thinks he knows better, is hipper to some better way of both playing QB and coaching. Mike Vanderjagt not only knocked Peyton, he knocked his coach, Tony Dungy, who is of this black faction that Rush cut out of the mob and claimed was getting a leg up on other coaches from the league and the media.

The Colts are now undefeated, going into Tampa Bay on Monday night. Regardless of the outcome of that game, there is little question that barring the unforeseen, within the next year, and then for the next five years or so, Manning and Dungy will play for the right to go to the Super Bowl a time or two, maybe even three. Dungy is stoically building another championship-level defense, just as he built the one in Tampa Bay, this time to complement the higher offensive skills of Manning. It's not a matter of the media or the league wanting or not wanting either one of them to do well, Rush. People (media is, surprisingly, made up of people) who cover the individual teams always want them to do well, whether they pretend objectivity or not; they want to cover good teams, winning teams, they want good teams to represent them, and the players and coaches who get hired in the NFL—getting hired being key, and this is what Rush was leaning toward, who gets hired, and is this affirmative action?—they either get it done, or they don't. The media does have its shortcomings. Propping up undeserving minorities is not one of them. Not after they are exposed as having shortcomings, anyway.

Fascinating.

McNabb said it was shocking.

Yeah? Wait until Donnie finds out that performance has nothing to with the so-called "social concern" Rush was talking about. Whatever somebody is accusing you of doing, nine times out of ten, that's what they are guilty of doing. McNabb can't play quarterback any better than Willie Mays played the outfield. And yet there were major-league teams, who were in the business of baseball, who did not sign Mays after trying him out. Now that's a social concern. All McNabb can do, for the time being, is play, and be glad to have the opportunity to play, because it didn't have to be that way. But it will be interesting to see what McNabb does in future years, how this impacts him.

How do I know this? Sometimes ESPN.com will sponsor a chat,

and invariably, with all the good sports questions that come in to me, there will be some that, how shall I say this, express "social concern." They accuse me of being racist, talk of how I and some of my occasional writing styles bring down the quality of writing for good educated people. Invariably, I will post one of those replies in the marathon chats, just to remind, not the readers, but myself, that some people can't get past color to performance, no matter what you do, no matter how well you perform. I know that I have forgotten more about composition than any of the hateful posters and their descendants will know in their lifetimes. And yet I end up defending my credibility again and again simply because of a trait I can't even see unless I look in a mirror.

That's the wrong Rush did, not to ESPN, not to the media, but to McNabb, McNair, Dungy. It's no matter, "moot" as McNabb said, that Rush can say he was simply questioning the so-called liberal media. Black coaches and quarterbacks who do not perform at the championship level in the NFL will be replaced soon enough, just as white ones will. But why foster resentment against the good black coaches and quarterbacks who perform, simply to get more attention from manipulated viewers of the very same media whose intentions you decry?

Rush's speculations were intriguing.

They were born of ego and power, and prey on suspicions and fears.

The great thing is that I can write this as well as think it.

I'm sorry Rush left so soon.

But to say "No mas" was the smart move.

It was about to get ugly.

Rush picked the wrong guy.

And I wish it was as simple as that.

—ESPN.com, October 3, 2003

WHY WE NEED
SPORTS NOW

Even the events of September 11 did not prevent Wiley from filing his ESPN.com column. In this powerful essay, he argues that the nation should once again turn to sports for healing, and, in one extraordinarily prescient passage, correctly surmised that there must have been some unknown athletes on Flight 93.

There comes a time when you're glad you know how to box—or know a damn good fighter.

This is one of those times.

There comes a time when football makes perfect sense.

This is one of those times.

There come certain times in Life On Earth when things get so bad, when the crap comes down so heavy, that all you can do is throw up your hands to the heavens and say, "Let us pray."

Eventually, in Life On Earth, people will try to tell you that religion or God is a vague concept at best, a medium used to hold down or delude or opiate people, an inferior concept to science, because science is pure. And you might even buy into all that for a while—up until some hurt and pain you know you aren't strong enough to handle alone comes down on you. Then you put in an emergency call. And it ain't to no 911. To God. *"Let us pray. Dear God . . ."*

There are other times when you need a break so bad, when you need to bow your neck and join in with your fellows so bad, that all you can do is look up at the scoreboard and ask, "What's the score?"

Eventually, in Life On Earth, people will try to tell you that sports is the toy shop, a mindless entertainment that exists basically to hold down or delude or opiate people, an inferior concept to business, because business is pure. And you might buy into all that for a while—up until some hurt or pain you know you aren't strong enough to handle alone comes down on you. Then you put in that emergency call. And it ain't to no bond trader. To the Home Team. *"What's the score? C'mon, guys . . ."*

Well . . . this is *both* of those times.

Think sports isn't like religion? Think again.

One of the spirited editors from this wacky bit of usually good-natured insanity called Page 2 is Jay Lovinger. Lovinger is older now, and as Richard Pryor once told us, "You don't get to be old being no fool." Sometimes, you don't get to be old anyway.

Lovinger just said something to me that sounded profound. We usually don't do profound on Page 2. But this ain't no usual time. Lovinger said, "For many, sports will be a big part of the healing process—or, at least, the forgetting or distracting. And don't underestimate the importance of that.

"People will talk about what there is to learn from this, about how we must then put those lessons into effect so that IT WILL NEVER HAPPEN AGAIN! IT MUST NEVER HAPPEN AGAIN!

"Bullcrap.

"There is nothing to be learned from this, other than:

"1.) There are some really crazy people out there; and

"2.) It is important to be lucky."

We're all lucky, those of us who made it through yesterday. Lucky we weren't on one of those four hijacked commercial jet airliners or in the World Trade Center towers or beneath them or at the Pentagon or in a grassy field in southwestern Pennsylvania.

We might be luckiest of all that we knew some of those people who were there, who took one for the team.

We're all in the Room of Rattled Consciousness now, with bats blowing saxophones, that place Muhammad Ali used to talk about, when you get hit with a haymaker, but can't lay down, or stay down, have to keep living, and keep fighting. Have to show up. Have to defend. Have to hit back to be respected.

This is when you're glad you know how to box, or know a boxer. This is when you care about outdated and uncivilized notions of self-defense. This is when you separate the men from the boys and the women from the girls, and when being 6-foot-8 and 260 chiseled pounds won't help you. The most important character traits in sports are not size and strength so much as they are poise and intelligence.

How many times during the eternity that was Tuesday, in the wake of the horrific jet bombings, the mass murders at the World Trade Center towers and The Pentagon, did we hear political or terrorism experts cry out for the need for "human intelligence"?

That's what separates the men and women from the boys and

girls in our microcosm of the world, too.

Know what? Maybe there actually was a great deal of human intelligence and poise displayed Tuesday, intelligence and poise that saved many lives.

We'll never know, but we honor it anyway.

Because it might have been.

And because it'll help fire us up and steel our resolve when we put it on the bulletin board before we go out to play the second half. Our turn.

What do I mean?

I mean this, and I mean it from the bottom of my heart: I believe there were Unknown Athletes on Flight 77 out of Dulles, bound for Los Angeles, and Flight 93 out of Newark, N.J., bound for San Francisco. The hijackers turned them into two D.C.-bound cruise missiles, the most powerful weapons of mass destruction next to the Halo Effect-tactical nukes. Those two planes didn't accomplish their missions.

Why?

What—or who—caused Flight 77 to hit ground first, diffusing most of its destructive energy before it slammed into the Pentagon? If Flight 77 hits the Pentagon flush, like Flight 175 out of Boston hit World Trade Center tower No. 2 at 9:08 a.m., then we don't have a Pentagon anymore. All we have left is a Right Angle.

And the Nut Case Hijackers didn't want to crash Flight 93 in a deserted field in Pennsylvania. They were headed for the U.S. Capitol Building Complex, or the White House. But Flight 93 never got there, so the Congress could stand on the steps of the Capitol and sing "God Bless America." If Flight 93 had made it to D.C., there wouldn't have been any steps to sing from, and not as many Congress people, either.

And my question is: Did somebody do something on either or both of those flights to prevent the worst from happening?

Somebody who was scared, somebody who knew he/she was probably gonna die—but did something anyway? Not a big something. Just enough of a move.

Maybe a stewardess who was stabbed but not dead yet tried to scratch the eyeball out of a head, and did, so Flight 77 bounced once before it hit the Pentagon.

Maybe some guy deadheading to S.F., some flight attendant, some gay guy, or some pilot, a former high school football bench-warmer, wrenched the controls away at just the right moment and planted Flight 93 in a field in Pennsylvania.

To me, that would be the height of athleticism . . . the greatest athlete is the one who can rescue a child from the fourth floor of a burning building; the greatest athlete is the one who can face four thugs in an alley and protect a couple of nurses and get them out of there, then disappear and not wait for credit.

A real player is somebody who never gives up, who keeps thinking all the way through, who's scared, damned right, but plays through being scared. The Heisman Trophy would not be enough for those kind, or for the Unknown Athletes on flights 77 and 93. Not even close enough.

There is something called the Congressional Medal of Honor that might do.

We'll never know. But we can *believe* we know. Sometimes, sports is like religion. And this *is* one of those times.

Of course the NFL should play its games this Sunday. It will get us in the mood to do what we have to do. No, it won't be pretty. Boxing, pro football, and War never are. But all can be made noble, depending on the bully, depending on the invading force, depending on the opponent, and what is being defended.

And by God and all that is Holy—and Sporting—this is one of those times.

—ESPN.com, September 12, 2001